**Philli Armitage-Mattin** has a passion for using Asian ingredients to create big flavour-filled meals. As a finalist on BBC One's *MasterChef: The Professionals 2020*, Philli entertained the nation with her take on playful Asian-inspired dishes.

Having studied for a master's degree in chemistry at Bristol University – she was first introduced to food science by the same research professor that worked with Heston Blumenthal – Philli went on to the University of West London to gain her professional cookery qualifications. She then worked in a Michelin-starred Japanese-inspired restaurant under the Gordon Ramsay Group, where she first learned how to use Asian ingredients.

Inspired by her love of Asian cuisine, Philli bought a one-way ticket to travel round Asia and experience the culture and food first-hand.

Her mission is to get people to try new flavours, using Asian ingredients such as miso and gochujang, and to make delicious dishes like Sichuan spiced lamb chops, Korean fried chicken burgers and shitake okonomiyaki (a Japanese savoury pancake).

*Taste Kitchen: Asia* is her first cookbook. Find Philli on her social channels @ChefPhilli or visit ChefPhilli.com.

# WELCOME TO YOUR TASTE KITCHEN

# TASTE KITCHEN: ASIA

# TASTE KITCHEN: ASIA

## PHILLI ARMITAGE-MATTIN

ROBINSON

To my best friend, cheerleader and partner, Tom: thank you for your endless support, excellent palate and for helping me organise my thoughts and the kitchen sink. This book wouldn't have happened without you.

# Contents

## COMFORT   112

## TARTY   154

## REFINED 186

## DARK HORSE 218

# INTRODUCTION

To me, the art of flavour is an obsession. Understanding how flavour is created is fundamental to making food we love to eat. Years of tasting, testing and experimenting have led me to discover how to craft excellent food every time by using an orchestra of ingredients that come together to create a harmony of flavour. As cooks, it's our job to balance these different tastes and make the flavours we love.

I have had so much fun on my journey with food, and I would like to share how my flavour obsession began.

## WHERE IT ALL BEGAN ...

I wasn't always familiar with the kitchen. I was brought up in the nineties and was extremely headstrong. I loved nothing more than a TV dinner made up of potato smiley faces, chicken nuggz and half a plate of tomato ketchup. We lived in America when I was young, and this is where I found my sweet tooth, when I was first introduced to Lucky Charms. For breakfast, I would insist on this high-energy, high-sugar cereal. I still love sugar and can admit I'm fully addicted; I still run around the flat full of energy until the inevitable sugar crash. Growing up, I noticed my mum didn't reach for the sweets, chocolates or biscuits; she didn't have a sugar monster inside her. Instead, while watching a movie, Mother would snack on unroasted, unsalted cashews or almonds. I found this strange. Why would she want to eat something without salt or sweetness? Then my dad, after a Sunday afternoon spent playing golf, would come back home to a cold beer and cheese and onion crisps – grim. Beer, bitter and intense, with the worst salty snack. I would wind him up by saying his breath smelled. We were all in the same environment, the same family, but we each had very different taste buds.

My love of food didn't start until I was a lot older, watching chefs like Gordon Ramsay on the telly working like dancers in the kitchen and producing dishes I could only imagine. Not knowing that in a few short years I would be working in one of his restaurants ... I had never tasted food like these chefs made before, but I was intrigued. Food was my happy place; it brought art, science and, most importantly, passion together. However, I was not always a good cook. It took years of experimentation, reading many cookbooks. When all the kids were

headed to the toy section of the department store, I'd be found in the middle of the kitchen department, wondering what all these gadgets and instruments did. I landed on baking, as many young teenage girls do. I would spend hours perfecting the macaron after many failed almond puddles, or trying to engineer cakes to look like ships or pigs. It was all about precision and science – and I could also go a bit crazy with glitter.

## EVERY DAY'S A SCHOOL DAY

At school, I was never great at English (I know, I've written a book – WTF!), but I loved science, maths and art. There was this new chef on TV called Heston Blumenthal, and he was using science in cooking, which I found fascinating. Learning about how cooking reactions occur on a molecular level and manipulating them to create something delicious – I was enthralled. Heston also playfully used flavour to create food memories. Later, while studying at Bristol, I was introduced to Peter Barham, who worked alongside Heston researching molecular gastronomy.

Following my formal education, and despite being warned against it by my friends and parents, I decided to follow my passion rather than my head. I landed my first chef role within the Gordon Ramsay Group while gaining my cooking qualifications. I thought my first experience with a professional kitchen would be creative, that I'd be making art, but you have none of that as an apprentice chef, and for a good reason. I have no clue what my 'dish ideas' would have been as a cocky twenty-two-year-old. I thought because I knew the theory of cooking, I could cook. But that's 100 per cent not the case; this is where the real learning began. The lesson of balancing flavour. I began to taste for salt, amend with lemon juice and vinegar, and refine with sugar. At the time, I did not appreciate it because I was getting the night bus back to my family home outside the M25 (thanks, Mum, for all those times you picked me up at 2 or 3 in the morning). On a weekly basis I would accidentally cut a finger, cry and proceed to faint – the struggle for flavour was real. In the beginning, my seasoning was way off; however, slowly, I would get the sweet reward of a nod of approval – or even just no comment – from my head chef after handing him/her a tasting spoon of the sauce or purée I had just slaved over for hours.

## SIX KEY PLAYERS

I discovered there are six key players in balancing a sauce or an overall dish: salty, sweet, spice, fat, tart and herby flavours. Different ingredients can be added to each of these flavours to change the balance. Add a bit more lemon juice for tarty flavour, balance it with olive oil or cream for fat; enhance all the flavours with salt, but not too much, and add spice for excitement, add sweetness for roundness and finish with soft herbs for floral notes. It was in an Asian-French restaurant, the second I'd worked in, that I first really got to grips with different misos, kombu, katsuobushi and shitake mushrooms. I began to understand the boldness and importance of the savoury taste: umami.

## FOLLOW THE YELLOW BRICK ROAD

After two years, I decided the restaurant kitchen was not for me, and I left on my yellow brick road for dreams of a 9–5, a spreadsheet, a desk chair and a cup of instant coffee. I landed a job designing ready meals for retail. What sold it to me was that I was able to be creative. Working in restaurant kitchens as a lower level chef, you're not allowed to create; that's for the head chef. I was extremely impatient; I wanted to create food. If you don't think this is sexy, fine, but I learned so much at my 'boring' 9–5, because UK ready meals do not allow the use of copious amounts of salt (thank you, government). As a chef, so much of what you're taught comes back to 'taste and season', and then probably add some more salt; in ready meals you're not allowed to do this. As my salt crutch was removed, I used my other six tastes to create flavourful food. These recipes were instructions followed to within 0.1g, and manufactured to create 6 tonnes of tikka masala sauce in a day, so they had to be correct. This is where I honed my understanding of the balance of spice. My teacher was Ren Patel, the spice queen herself. She would use spice like an artist, using base-note spices like turmeric, cumin and coriander during the beginning of cooking so they have time to marry with the other ingredients, and flavouring with high-note spices like cinnamon and garam masala at the end, just like finishing a classic French butter sauce with lemon juice.

I loved Asian flavours and wanted to learn more. What better way to do this than to book a one-way ticket to Japan and spend the year working, travelling, cooking and eating my way across East and South East Asia? I got to learn about all kinds of different ingredients, noticing how the gochujang in Seoul and doubanjiang in Xi'an have similar characteristics, and the XO sauce in Hong Kong and the rayu in Osaka played similar roles in dishes. However, **I linked these ingredients by flavour rather than by region.**

## FLAVOUR BALANCE

You have this book so I'm guessing you're into Asian flavours as well. My aim is to introduce you to the art of balancing flavour, to show you how to taste your ingredients, adjust recipes and add to the overall flavour profile of a dish.

When you know how flavour works and feel the urge to add a little chilli oil to your spag bol or kimchi to your big mac, that's totally okay. **If it's yummy for you, or whoever you're cooking for, that's all that matters.**

The scientific foundation of this book is based on my own food science journey. The beauty of science is that new theories are always emerging and hypotheses are being proven or disproven. I encourage you to challenge the theory of the science and conduct your own home experiments.

I am not pretending that these recipes are traditional. If they were, you would need to go to these individual villages and towns and find scarce, specific ingredients your local supermarket doesn't stock. Instead, over years of testing and refining recipes, I have added the minimum amount of ingredients to get the maximum flavour in the most efficient way for home cooks. If you can't find a specific ingredient, there are substitutes. There are shortcuts and hacks, so if you want to make your dumplings and wrappers, that is cool; however, if you want to buy some ready-made, that's fine too. I understand that sometimes we have 90 minutes to create something exquisite, but other times we only have 10 minutes. After reading and cooking these recipes, you will have learned how to train your palate to notice a dish's flavour and balance. **One of the most important techniques I can teach you is to taste as you go along and keep on tasting,** spoon pot at the ready. Amend and adjust and make notes. This book is your personal recipe journal, here to help you on your journey to cook for your taste.

 Welcome to your Taste Kitchen

# What is taste and what is flavour?

We've all heard of taste and taste buds, right? There are five tastes you sense through your tongue, and that you can only taste on your tongue.

However, we often hear the terms flavour and taste used inter-changeably, when actually flavour is completely multisensory and encompasses everything from smell, sight and sound to touch, memory and feeling. It's really hard to describe flavour because it's our brain piecing together a puzzle with missing information, while our memory and expectation fills in the gaps. Flavour is a multi-sensory complex phenomenon. Research psychologist Charles Spence has heavily researched this topic and coined the term gastrophysics.

The five basic tastes – sweet, sour, bitter, salty and umami – can be detected by your tongue. It was previously reported that different parts of the tongue detect different tastes; however, this is widely believed to have been disproven and many believe the tongue map to be false.

**COULD YOU BE PAID TO EAT?**

All the tongue's receptors can taste all the basic tastes. The receptors are mainly on the edges of the tongue with none in the middle. You might have heard of supertasters, the people that have high sensitivity to bitter flavours. If you are a supertaster, you could have the prerequisites to become a professional taster, people who taste chocolate or coffee as their job and have their tongue insured for millions of pounds. If you're dreaming about being paid to eat chocolate all day and wonder if you're a supertaster, it is generally tested by sensitivity to bitter compounds. So, if you hate Brussels sprouts, coffee or 90 per cent dark choc, you could be a supertaster. There is also found to be a link between psychopathic tendencies and bitter and spicy food, although I don't believe one is caused by the other … Our mood can affect flavour too: when you've had a meal with your family and there's an argument at the dining table, no matter the flavour, the food will not taste as good and will often leave a bitter taste on your tongue.

## SMELLS DELICIOUS

You might associate flavour with the taste on your tongue; however, the majority of the flavour actually comes from receptors in our nose, the olfactory receptors. If you describe a food as smoky, fruity or herbal you are actually using the olfactory receptors to sense the flavour of these volatile compounds. There is a simple way to test your nose receptors: by eating a jelly bean and holding your nose tightly closed, you will taste the sweetness but little else. Once you release your nose, the flavour of the lemon, strawberry or grape come into play. We smell by two methods, breathing the aroma in, then once again when we have chewed the food releasing different compounds. For example, have you ever wondered why blue cheese smells bad but once you allow it to melt on your tongue its umami creaminess is delicious? Or how the smell of a bag of freshly ground coffee is very different to the end cup?

We can distinguish more than a trillion different odours, and we generate new scent neurons every few weeks to make sure our sense is in good working order. However, as we age, we tend to lose our sense of smell.

We all taste and smell differently. This is most prevalent in the coriander phenomenon – do you find it soapy or fragrant? Our unique genetics are responsible for the majority of us sensing that coriander is fragrant; however, if you believe it tastes like soap this is a clear example of us perceiving flavour differently.

Smell evokes powerful emotion, and is also used in various successful marketing strategies. There's a reason you can smell Subway from down the street, or you'll know if you're ever near an Abercrombie & Fitch store. The majority of money made by a cinema is from the concessions sold, not the tickets. There's a reason the first thing you notice is the smell of the popcorn. If you're a little bit hungry, smell can also trigger you to get hangry when you walk past a Maccy D's.

## LOOKS AS GOOD AS IT TASTES

Even more powerful is the way our brain processes sight. The way food looks heavily impacts the perceived flavour, and looking at food makes us salivate, which is in turn flavour-inducing. Ugly food doesn't make us hungry. There's a reason why there is so much food porn on social media. It's scary that there is a link between BMI and people that view unhealthy food on social media; it could be because these people (myself included) are scrolling through oozing egg yolks and dripping burgers rather than putting their running shoes on. The trick to perceived flavour is making food look enticing, and the trick on social media is to make it look high energy and in motion, which makes it look fresh – #yolkporn ticks both boxes! Check my Egg and Bacon Nasi Goreng for an example of this (p. 138).

Flavour perception through viewing food is based on food memories: if you've never tasted a raspberry before but you know how strawberries and blackberries taste, then you could assume the raspberry would be tart, sweet and fruity, and you would be correct. You do this all the time subconsciously. Therefore, with this theory we can find a link between colour and flavour: pinkish-red can be sweet while light yellow-green is sour and light blue is salty. There is also a link between shapes and flavours. We generally link more angular shapes to sour, spicy and salty food, hence why pubs serve their salted chips on a black slate. In contrast, round, unthreatening shapes are more associated with rich, fatty, sweet food. Generally, we like colour contrast in plating, so if you're serving a vanilla panna cotta maybe choose a darker plate or make a strawberry sauce to go with it.

## CRISPY OR FRIED?

Crunchy and crispy are the terms most used by marketing companies to make us buy food; think 'crispy chicken tenders' instead of 'fried'. Watch *Super Size Me 2* to find out more. We love crunchy food because we associate crunch with freshness – it's so much more satisfying to break a crispy Pringle than bend a stale one. **We actually hear the crunch rather than feel it;** it's conducted through our jaw bones and through the air if our mouth is open. It's the same as when bubbles pop in a fizzy drink. Crunch is correlated to high energy-density foods as the majority of crunchy food has been dehydrated quickly in oil (frying) rather than the low and slow dry heat dehydration.

Like we associate different colours with different sounds, we also pair higher-pitched sounds with sweeter flavours and lower notes with bitter, deeper flavour. Food would not be quite the same without sound. Think of bacon sizzling in a pan; next time you're cooking bacon or mushrooms listen for this sound of the steam evaporating. As the sizzle noises change, this is the last of the water turning to vapour and then the heat increases, rising to temperatures that caramelise the sugars and proteins. Use all your senses when cooking: hear the pan as well as watch it.

The dish most famously paired with sounds is Heston Blumenthal's 'Sounds of the Sea'. One of the first dining experiences to use sonic seasoning, an iPod played seaside sounds while you ate the dish, transporting you to a British seaside town with seagulls and crashing waves. This was so innovative for the time and is one of the reasons I became a chef. The dish evolved out of an experiment executed by Charles Spence and Heston, who looked at how the flavour of egg and bacon ice cream changed by playing bacon sizzling sounds and farmyard music; unsurprisingly the ice cream tasted more eggy when listening to farmyard sounds, and more bacony when the sound of sizzling bacon was played, even though this was the same ice cream. A further experiment was conducted eating oysters with farmyard music and sounds of the British seaside; the oysters eaten with seaside sounds were found to be more pleasant. I interpreted this dish on *MasterChef* and was lucky enough to taste it for myself this year, which was like being in a time capsule and showed the evolution of multisensory dining.

**FEELING OUR FOOD**

Burgers are great, yes? They're indulgent, high-cal deliciousness. However, we also eat them with our hands (well, most of us; those knife and fork burger-eaters need to have a long hard look at themselves in the mirror). We feel the brioche bun squish in our hands and the juicy burger might spill a few drips on our neck-tucked napkin, or a bit of sauce may cover the side of your chin; this is all the experience of tactile flavour.

We feel the texture of food as we chew (masticate) and feel the food breaking down. Some people might like the flavour of

foods like mushrooms, but the texture can sometimes be a problem. We feel viscosity with our tongue, like rich velvety sauces or ice creams. Generally, the increase in viscosity reduces the amount we detect volatile compounds.

The trigeminal system detects pain, the sense that's used when you feel a pan is burning hot, and can sense on your tongue when a food is spicy or minty. Personally, I can't handle super minty toothpastes, but my spice tolerance goes up to a Nando's medium heat before I need to reach for the sour cream and chive.

**OUR FOOD MEMORIES**

A sense that we don't normally think about impacting flavour is our memory. Have you tried to feed a child green peas? Because they hate broccoli, which is also green, they predict they will taste the same so they won't like the peas. This is our expectation of flavour, and it plays a part when people won't try different foods because of their memory of something similar which they found disagreeable. We are born liking the sweet umami flavours found in breast milk, however we naturally avoid salty, sour, bitter and spicy foods. Some of our flavour preferences are learned during the latter stages of pregnancy, while we're still in the womb. How we know whether we like or dislike a food is down to our recollection of the flavour. We learn that some foods or drinks deliver sugar, fat or alcohol to the body and therefore learn to like certain foods. For example, when you had that first sip of beer you might not have thought it tasted so great, however we generally like the effect it has on our evenings so learn to like the bitter drink.

Our memory helps us choose dishes on a menu that we predict we'll enjoy and is key to how we recall our likes and dislikes. It has been researched that we recall the beginning and end of a meal far more than the dishes served in the middle, and we forget the meal flavours fairly easily. We remember social and theatrical events more than the flavours in a dish. If you want to make a great memorable meal try serving something shocking, funny or exciting or entertain for a birthday, anniversary and Christmas.

I love trying new flavours, that's what inspires me. I encourage you to taste the dishes with your tongue, nose, eyes, ears, (clean) fingers and memory and be open to tasting and cooking differently.

# What's your taste?

We all have different personality types that we recognise, and so do our taste buds. However, we often don't take time to think about how we use flavour to give ourselves maximum enjoyment. Each of us enjoys flavours differently. The problem is that the majority of us do not understand which individual flavours are going to satisfy and tantalise our own unique palates.

Taste buds are the receptors that trigger the sensation of taste, and they are part of what make up our palate, or flavour worlds. Our palate can change with our mood or even the weather, and we can also have more than one palate. We all have different flavour worlds and experience flavours differently; for example, women can differentiate smells better than men and you lose your sense of smell as you age. The dishes in the book are therefore grouped by flavour profile and emotion. My aim is for you to cook more confidently, using these flavours in your everyday cooking.

## WHAT'S YOUR PALATE?

The flow chart opposite will guide you towards your palate type; however, please remember this is just a guide and your palate is not fixed; you may find that you enjoy a combination of flavours that work for you.

The tastes are split into six types. Later on, I will show you how different flavours can create balanced dishes to satisfy these six palates. Some of the recipes featured in this book may include several prominent flavours at once, but once you understand the six palates and your own preferences, you'll be able to dial up or down your ingredients to suit you and make each recipe individual to you.

# What's your palate?

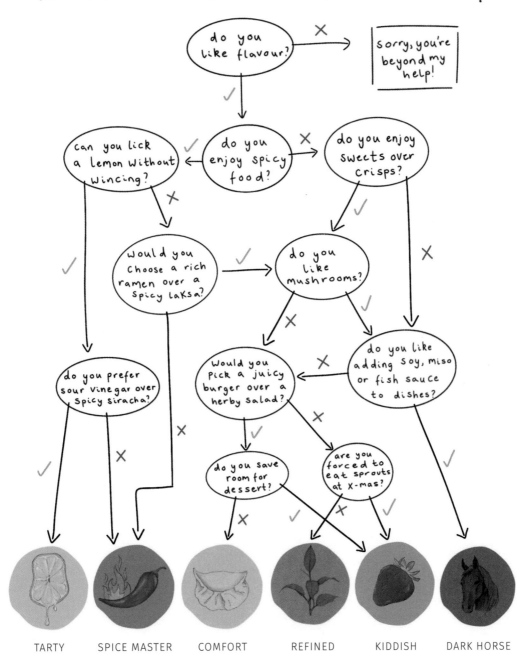

do you like flavour? ✗ → sorry, you're beyond my help!

✓

do you enjoy spicy food?

can you lick a lemon without wincing? ✓ ←

✗ do you enjoy sweets over crisps?

✗ Would you choose a rich ramen over a spicy laksa?

✓ do you like mushrooms?

✓ ✗

do you prefer sour vinegar over spicy siracha?

Would you pick a juicy burger over a herby salad?

✗ do you like adding soy, miso or fish sauce to dishes?

do you save room for dessert?

are you forced to eat sprouts at x-mas?

TARTY    SPICE MASTER    COMFORT    REFINED    KIDDISH    DARK HORSE

## TARTY

Tarty is about bold, cheeky flavour. When you have added a little too much lime to your Sunday smashed avo and you feel the sides of your cheeks tingle with the sharp acidity – that's Tarty. It's flavour that literally makes you smile. You'll find sour Disco Pickles (p. 158), Gunpowder Pots (p. 168) and tangy Yuzu Lemon Tart(ish) (p. 183).

## SPICE MASTER

The king or queen of the local curry house, the Spice Master can order a vindaloo or even a phall without breaking a sweat. The Spice Master loves an Aubergine Vindaloo (p. 92), a Chilli Oil (p. 50) (whack it on!), and raging hot Tteok-Bokki (Korean-Inspired) Spicy Cheesy Rice Cakes p. 82). Spice doesn't just come in chillies; you can also find a milder heat in radish, watercress, rocket and ginger.

## COMFORT

Comfort is all that you crave on a cold evening or after a big night out. We're talking indulgent food that hugs you from the inside. This is one of my favourite palates: it's Cuddly Dan Dan Noods (p. 136), My Squishy Bao buns (p. 140), and the BBBR (Brown Butter Basmati Rice, p. 130).

## REFINED

efined is a grown-up flavour,
ith hints of bitterness and
erby flavour. If you like a
ark green leafy veg, you'll
ove the Crispy Kale and
quash with Satay Sauce
. 200), and if you don't
hink coriander tastes like
oap, there's Spicy Green Fish
akes (p. 204), Coriander and
oconut Chicken Curry
. 208) or Green Curry
lussels (p. 206).

## KIDDISH

If you can down a bag of
gummy bears in one like me,
your tastes are a bit kiddish.
I'm not calling you childish;
there's no shame in loving ice
cream! It's all about sweet
food; not necessarily over-
the-top sweet candyfloss, but
high-colour, high-energy food.
You're into a Korean Fried
Chicken Burger (p. 64) with
bright red gochujang glaze,
or fluffy Japanese Cheesecake
(p. 72), and you always lick
the bowl clean. Welcome to
Kiddish.

## DARK HORSE

Dark Horse is a savoury
flavour that is the background
to most cooking. We're all
secretly addicted to this
flavour, even if you don't
know it yet! The Dark Horse is
deep, rich Fish Sauce Chicken
Wings (p. 228); Shitake
Okonomiyaki (p. 232) and
deep Cheat XO Sauce (p. 255).

# How to use this book

I urge you to deep dive into each chapter. As you start to cook some of these recipes you'll get an understanding of each palate. You'll notice that the recipes in each of the chapters rely on broadly similar ingredients so that your weekly shop will be a little easier, whether you're cooking for a Spice Master or a connoisseur of Refined flavours.

## THE FLAVOUR WHEEL

With each recipe there is a corresponding flavour wheel. The wheel depicts the balance of flavour for each recipe. I have designed each recipe to be suited to the palate in that chapter and so they are delicious as is, but the beauty of all the recipes is that they can be adapted to suit *every* taste.

You have started to delve into your individual palate. When cooking a recipe from *Taste Kitchen*, I would like you to decide how your taste buds are feeling today and be mindful of your flavour world. Each ingredient within the recipe will play a part in the balance of flavour of that recipe. In each recipe, there will be a stage where I mention **'taste adjust'**. At this moment I want you to pause, take your spoon, dunk it into the sauce you're cooking and taste. Think about the flavour, and which ingredients are playing a certain role in the flavour balance. Chilli adds heat but that can be balanced with fat, like cream, or acid, like lemon, and you always need depth from savoury flavours, like soy or miso (umami bombs). Within each wheel section you will find an ingredient that is providing the flavour for each palate in that recipe. If you've tasted your sauce and decided you want something more Tarty, whack a bit more acid in; more Spice Master, sprinkle in the chilli; more Kiddish, load in the sugar. I want each recipe to be yours so that you start to think like a Taste Kitchen cook and learn to question the recipes that you've been cooking for years.

Remember, the balance of flavour is an art and training your palate takes time. You won't get it right the first time, but that's okay, you'll get another chance tomorrow. It's a journey and, if you're like me, you weren't born a great cook. I cooked and tasted and cooked again. It took years to train my palate. My aim is to shortcut this training and guide you through flavour: learning the art of salting, building depth in rich umami layers and how to add a squeeze of lime juice at the very last minute to lift all the other flavours.

*Fancy*

Some recipes are a little bit fancier than others – they are extra special because they take a little more effort or have a few more ingredients. I want you to save these recipes for when you have more time or someone to impress.

GIVE IT
A TRY!!

## QR CODES

There are certain skills that I would like to teach you but that might not be as easy to describe in words or with pictures. Personally, I'm a visual learner, so I need a video. Scan the QR code to gain that skill and up your cooking game.

## THE SAUCE

Sauces, or condiments, are your secret powerhouse to add a flavour punch to any dish. They have the ability to lift a dish and make it super enjoyable for any fussy eater. I love condiments so channel your inner condiment king or queen and make your own. You'll find my favorite condiment recipes near the back of the book. If you don't have time to whip up a chutney there are now so many great quality sauces you can grab from the local markets.

## COMMUNITY

Okay, so now that you have this book you'll see that I've tried to write it with your questions in mind, adding extra nuggets of information where possible. However, there might be something you're confused about or you need to know where to get an ingredient. Fear not! Hit me a comment on my social media @chefphilli and I'll try to answer where possible. But can I ask a favour? If you see a question from a fellow *Taste Kitchen* cook in the comments, help them out if you know the answer.

# Taste Kitchen: Pantry

If you're in the supermarket and you can't find a particular ingredient, or if you're simply not a fan of something, don't worry, there's always a substitute. I've tried to keep the ingredient list fairly simple throughout the recipes, only calling for specific ingredients where absolutely necessary. Listing ingredients into specific palates will give you an insight into how each flavour profile is driven by certain ingredients.

The ingredients in bold are the ingredients that are pretty much essential and that I always have to hand. They're not listed below, but you should always have some shallots, onions and garlic at the ready too!

## KIDDISH

**White sugar** or caster sugar or rock sugar

**Brown sugar**, jaggery or palm sugar

**Honey** or maple syrup

**Mirin** or 1:1 ratio white rice vinegar and sugar

Kejap manis or Sticky Soy Glaze (p. 248)

Hoisin sauce

## SPICE MASTER

**Fresh chillies**, red and green

**Thai chillies** or rocket finger chillies

Dried chilli powder, chilli flakes, whole dried chillies or gochugaru

**Sriracha** or Funky Chilli Sauce (p. 249)

Sichuan peppercorns, sancho pepper or Sichuan oil

**Philli's Chilli Oil** (p. 250) or shop-bought Chilli oil or Lao Gan Ma chilli crisp

**Gochujang** or 1:1 ratio miso and sriracha

Galangal, horseradish or ginger

Doubanjiang

Togarashi or 1:1 ratio chilli powder and sesame seeds

## COMFORT

**Tahini** or peanut butter or any nut butter

**Cooking oils:** vegetable oil, rapeseed oil, canola oil, sunflower oil or peanut oil

**Dressing oils:** olive oil or sesame oil, truffle oil or cold-pressed rapeseed oil

**Coconut milk,** coconut cream or soy cream

**Butter**, ghee, coconut oil or goose fat

**Rice flour** or glutinous rice flour

**Cornflour**, potato starch or tapioca starch

**Sesame seeds** or nuts

**Fresh noodles** (p. 96), soba noodles, udon noodles, egg noodles or rice noodles

## TARTY

**Rice vinegar** or Chinese black vinegar

**White wine vinegar** or white vinegar

**Sake**

**Tamarind or lime juice**

**Lime or lemon juice**

**Yuzu or lemon juice**

Shaoxing wine or sherry

Lemongrass or lemon zest

Kafir lime leaves or lime zest

## REFINED

**Spring onions**, chives or garlic chives

**Coriander**

Thai basil, holy basil or basil

Parsley

Mint

Curry leaves

Shiso leaves

## DARK HORSE

**White miso** or red miso

**Fish sauce** or shrimp paste

**Parmesan cheese** or pecorino

**Soy sauce** or tamari

Dried shitake mushrooms or porcini powder

MSG, nutritional yeast or katsuobushi

# Put down the tiny knife

Not many people talk about which knives are actually used in professional kitchens, and, let me be honest, there are too many times when I go over to a friend's house and they're using a steak knife for butternut squash: it makes me want to scream into a pillow.

There are a few essentials that every home chef needs in their set. I have a whole collection of knives because certain knives do certain jobs in cooking but there are actually only two or three I use daily. And please, always use a sharp knife – there will be fewer accidents and less blood spilt!

## THE COOK'S BABY

I find knives a bit like shoes or cars; the more expensive they are the more beautiful they tend to be, but also the more love, care and attention they need. You wouldn't use a Ferrari for the school run or an off-road adventure; likewise, you'll want to be careful not to chip or blunt your knife by using it for the wrong reason, nor would you let it rust.

Every knife has great qualities and drawbacks. European-style knives like Henckels, Sabatier, Dick and Wüstof have an edge between 20–40 degrees. They're made from super tough steel, which means they're hard and resistant to scratching and damage. However, a Japanese-style knife is made by layering Damascus steel and is a lot thinner and sharper at around 15–25 degrees. It can easily slice through any vegetable and meat, damaging the ingredient less, but it can be prone to chips so must be stored carefully and sharpened more regularly.

There is less force needed when slicing across versus chopping vertically as you are slicing through cells rather than using the chopping force. The force needed for chopping is twice as much as is needed for slicing sideways, because slicing creates a microscopic serrated surface and the roughness catches, causing friction to generate a shearing force. However, some ingredients are prone to fracturing – like cheese or carrots – so require a chopping force; do not use your baby on ingredients like these unless you want a blunt knife. A blunt knife edge only relies on chopping force so more energy is needed, and accidents are more likely.

I would invest in an 18–25cm/7–10in chef's knife you love. When I got my first Japanese knife I went into a real shop and held different knives in my hand to feel the weight of the knife, the size and how it feels in your cutting style. When you have the perfect knife in your hand, you'll know it feels right.

## THE MVP

I'll let you in on a little secret: in just about every professional kitchen the knife that gets used the most only costs around £40, and many chefs use it as their main knife. The Victorinox pastry knife is probably the most versatile, most-used knife I own; it's great for your Sunday brunch, slicing a pie, cutting through pork crackling, as well as dicing an onion. The serrated blade stays sharp for ages and saws through cells quickly and easily so is super efficient. Ideally you should use a beautifully sharp Japanese blade for herbs, but if I don't have anything sharp to hand this knife always does a great job.

## PARING KNIFE

It's not completely essential but I do love a paring knife for opening packets, removing garlic cloves and other little, fiddly jobs.

## THE WORKHORSE

This is probably a knife that gets overlooked. You need a knife in your selection that's heavy and capable of chopping through that thick butternut and breaking through joints of chicken. A knife that will take the hit and effectively protect your beautiful cook's baby. A real workhorse: give it a quick swish on a knife-honing steel then crack on.

## MANDOLINE

I use a mandoline to get a really fine slice. No matter how good your knife skills are, it's quicker and easier, and produces more consistent results, to use a mandoline to slice something super thin. Caveat: they're a little dangerous so always use a guard. If you don't want to invest in one you can use a speed peeler for turning carrots into ribbons.

## CHOPPING BOARD

So now you have a great knife. Great! But if you have a crappy chopping board, your knife is going to suck pretty quickly, dulling the sharp edge. A thick wooden chopping board about 40cm/16in wide will be your friend and keep your kitchen organised. The second-best option here would be soft plastic, like those used in professional kitchens, as they can be bunged in the dishwasher. I generally use a wooden board for most prep and then swap to a plastic for raw meat preparation. I never use a glass or granite chopping board as they are harder than your knife and therefore blunt the edge very quickly.

## WHETSTONE/KNIFE STEEL

It is vitally important to keep your knives in good condition and ensure they are sharp. Always keep them dry to prevent rust and rub a little oil on the blade with kitchen paper after it has dried.

To sharpen I normally use a whetstone in between sending them to a knife sharpening service. Sharpening stones have different grits; the higher the number the finer the grit. I use a combination stone, 1000–3000 to get the edge and 6000 to polish and finish. You start with a medium grit to get a knife edge and then polish it to refine the edge.

Coarse stones – less than 1000 grit

Medium stones – between 1000 and 3000 grit

Finishing stones – between 4000 and 8000 grit

I also use a diamond steel or ceramic knife sharpener just to keep my knife sharp throughout the day.

HOW TO SHARPEN YOUR KNIFE

# Set yourself up for success

The main difference I see between a professional chef and a home cook is a little organisation. Now this comes with time in the kitchen, but there are a few shortcuts that I would love you to try out and see how efficient your cooking becomes.

### THE SPOON POT

In *every* pro kitchen you'll find that next to a chef's workspace there's a pot of spoons. This is because the chef is *always tasting* and you should be too. Flavour is about balance, and these recipes will help you understand that, but you need to taste as this is the fundamental technique of all cooking. Before you next start cooking, make sure you place some spoons inside a cup of water to keep them clean. Then taste, taste and taste again.

### DOUBLE SALT PIG

Salt is the backbone of flavour. Always have both fine salt and flaky salt to hand to make sure you're seasoning and building layers throughout your cooking process with fine salt, and then finishing with flaky salt.

### J-CLOTH

These little cloths are excellent. Use a damp cloth underneath your chopping board to make sure it's secure, and a second folded one to wipe down your chopping board and the blade of your knife in between jobs. Also, if you want to rest a piece of meat, whack it on a clean J-cloth to stop it dripping everywhere.

### MICROPLANE

Probably my second most-used piece of kitchen equipment. If you're mincing garlic or ginger – which I do a lot – I always use a microplane. It's just a quick grate straight into the pan and the clean-up is super quick, rather than faffing around with those garlic presses. It's also great for zesting lemons or limes, shaving Parmesan or, if you've accidentally burnt the edge of a tart or pork skin, just taking off the burnt bit.

## METAL TONGS

A good pair of metal tongs is perfect for nearly every kitchen job. I use thin, long ones that are nimble and accurate. They're going to protect your hands as you toss noodles, sear steaks and gently turn roasties. Just make sure you get ones that are long enough.

## DIGITAL MEAT PROBE AND POKEY STICKS

A meat probe is a foolproof way to make sure you get everything juicy and fully cooked. I use a digital one to get an instant read on the temperature. It's also great for poking veggies; if there's a little resistance, then you know the veggies are just cooked. You can also use pokey sticks (small metal olive picks) – this is what a lot of pro chefs use to check the doneness of their meats. Simply poke the metal stick into the meat, then wait a second, remove and place it on the underside of your wrist. If it feels cold it's lower than your body temp (about 37°C) and the meat needs more cooking. If it feels hot then it's way hotter than your body and is overcooked. If it feels warm it's just right at a little hotter than your body, hopefully around 45°C.

As a rule of thumb, I generally look to hit the following temperatures when cooking:

◆ 45–50°C for most fish. The fish proteins denature at 40°C so at any higher temperature the albumin starts to come out of the fish (that white stuff that comes out of the fish during cooking).

◆ 45–50°C for quick-cooking meat like steaks, lamb racks and pork loin, then allow to rest to 54–57°C for perfect medium rare steak because the myosin has denatured but the myoglobin (the red colour) has not.

◆ 63–65°C for poultry breast: you need to take it to a higher temp to kill any bad bacteria. Chicken thigh meat should be cooked for longer and to much higher temperatures (80–90°C) to make sure the gelatin breaks down.

◆ 80–91°C for slow meat braises like short ribs or pork belly, to make sure the gelatin and fat is broken down. Lower oven temperatures (140°C) ensure a softer, more juicy texture.

## SMALL OVEN TRAYS

When I'm prepping ingredients, I love using tiny oven trays to keep parts of my prep on rather than using a thousand tiny bowls. Just prep everything before into small piles on one tray and then scoop out what you need for each part of the recipe; it also means there's less washing-up and you're more organised. They're also great for resting meat and fried chicken on before serving.

## DIGITAL SCALES

I normally weigh everything on digital scales as it's the most accurate way of measuring quantities, especially for lighter ingredients.

## PLASTIC BENCH SCRAPER

Super cheap – they'll only set you back £1 – and not only useful when portioning dough but great for getting all the crumbs off your work surface.

## TIMER

Please use something to keep an eye on your oven. We all have a million things we're doing on a daily basis, and the last thing you want is a charcoal dinner.

## MEASURING SPOONS (AND MY RELATIONSHIP WITH THEM)

I don't like measuring spoons; the first time I used them properly is for this book. The reason I hate them is they're awful to clean and there's always only one of each, so you're constantly washing. I prefer to use a standard eating tablespoon from my spoon pot. Now a standard eating tablespoon is about half a proper measuring tablespoon so, if you're like me and prefer to use a standard tablespoon, double the number of standard eating spoons stated in the recipe. The same goes for teaspoons. However, if you love your measuring spoons I'd get a couple of sets to prevent the constant washing-up.

### CHEEKY WHISK

Tiny whisks or magi-whisks are excellent for emulsifying and stirring any sauce or dressing together. They generally live in my spoon pot too.

### TINY STEP SPATULA

These mini spatulas are great for poking and turning meat, fish and vegetables. They're also amazing for making sandwiches as they are the ultimate spreader. They have a place in my spoon pot.

### TINY SILICON SPATULA

Super useful to get into the edges of a saucepan to scrape out that last little bit. I like to use black silicon so that it doesn't stain when I'm making a turmeric curry.

### BOWLS AND TINY BOWLS

Always have a selection of bowls for batters and tiny bowls for sauces and dressings. I normally use the IKEA aluminium ones as they're cheap, light and conduct heat fairly well.

### CAST-IRON AND HEAVY FRYING PANS

A heavy frying pan is key to getting enough heat in the pan to beautifully sear a steak, chicken thighs or a boatload of mushrooms.

A cast-iron pan retains heat really well and is a good conductor; this means once you add your protein to the pan it won't cool it down as much and it will take less energy to increase the temp to create caramelisation. The Maillard reaction, a reaction between sugar and proteins that creates the perfect caramelised crust, occurs at 154°C, so you need a hot pan.

They are also ovenproof so no need to preheat an oven tray. A good cast-iron pan will last for years and the more you use it the more seasoned (non-stick) it becomes. I have mine passed down from my parents and as it's so well-loved I can use less oil. The downside is they do rust and are super heavy.

Another common option is a heavy non-stick three-layer pan, which has all the benefits of non-stick but is more durable than Teflon, cheaper than copper and lighter than cast iron. They aren't always ovenproof though, and you should be careful when washing them to make sure you don't scratch the coating. I like to find a medium-weight pan with a lid so I can sear and steam dumplings and veggies.

## WOK

I love my wok. Get yourself one. They're super versatile – stir-frying, stewing, deep-frying, they do it all.

## TINY BLENDER AND STICK BLENDER

You need something to blend things with in your kitchen. A blender is great for making emulsions and batters as well as a curry paste, if you don't want to slave over a pestle and mortar for ages. Yes, a curry paste is better made by grinding but let's be honest: I'm too impatient for that.

## STAND MIXER

I only use my inherited 60s Kenwood stand mixer for baking recipes like the Miso Sticky Toffee Pudding (p. 244) and Japanese Cheesecake (p.72) as they're not the same with just mixing by hand (especially the cheesecake). All my other dough mixes, dumplings, noodles and bao I normally mix with chopsticks – less to wash up.

# Don't fear NaCl

Salt or sodium chloride (NaCl) has a bad rep and I'm here to guide you through your fear of salt. If your doctor has told you that you are consuming too much, yes, you should cut down; however, salt is an essential mineral that we need to survive and, more importantly in my mind, it is the key building block of flavour.

The main difference I see between home and professional kitchens is the way we salt food. This is an easy fix to get your kitchen and food feeling and tasting a little more pro. The way we salt is really important. I'm guessing you normally reach into the salt pig and use your thumb and your index finger to grab a light pinch of fine salt to sprinkle on the end of your cooking, or, worse, a few cracks of the salt grinder on the table having not seasoned throughout your cooking process at all. Salt is a flavour enhancer, so let me share how you can build layers of flavour throughout your cooking.

## SEASON TO TASTE

As a chef, one of your first lessons is how to season food. This is my version of that lesson, for you. Next to my salt pots I have a spoon pot, because you should sprinkle salt and then taste again. This is because a few grains of salt can be the difference between a good plate of food and a great one. I can't stress this enough: always keep tasting and your taste buds will train themselves. You'll know when the seasoning is just right when all the other flavours in a sauce pop and you can feel them all working together, enhancing the butteriness, sweetness and acid. Just at the very last minute, squeeze over some lemon juice and crush some flaky sea salt, then you've really smashed it.

The amount of salt required for a dish varies, and the action you need to take will be different. To have the most control, use the three-finger pinch. It's simple enough to do this: just grasp a full pinch of fine salt between your index finger, middle finger and thumb. Allow the grains of salt to fall gently through the space between your fingers over your food. A phrase that will be familiar to many chefs is 'season from a height'; if you're sprinkling salt close to a piece of protein or vegetables you will be seasoning in a very confined area, whereas if you raise your hand to Salt Bae heights, you will get an even coverage over the protein or vegetables.

I like to have two different salts in my kitchen. The first is a fine salt, which is made up of small grains. These are low cost and, due to their size, they dissolve quickly into a liquid. The other salt is what restaurants call 'finishing salt', beautiful, natural, flaky sea salt that is used to finish off a dish. You might have seen chefs crushing the salt crystals between their fingers over seared meats, brownies or crispy potatoes just before they go to the table. They add a sweet seasoning as well as a little textured crunch. In England we often use Maldon or Dorset sea salt; in France, there's Fleur de Sel; in the US there's Jacobsen Salt Co and, shout out to my friend Matt Broussard @ACookNamedMatt, who launched his own brand. I once used a salt in Japan that was so big each grain was almost the size of a stamp and came in their own presentation box – next level. I have two salts in little pots next to the hob so I can lovingly grab a pinch for seasoning my food.

Salt needs to be layered and built up over time in your saucepan, as it needs time to dissolve through vegetables and meats. The lower the concentration of water the longer the meat or vegetable needs to be salted as it takes longer for the salt to dissolve and move through osmosis. Osmosis is a process where two different concentrations of solution find equilibrium through a semipermeable membrane – i.e. the salty brine and the non-salty chicken breast try to get to the same concentration so the salt enters the meat.

Meats tend to be lower in water content than fish or vegetables, the tougher meats like shoulder or belly being the lowest concentrations. This is because they contain a lot of fat and it's harder for the salt to transport itself through fat. So meats that take a long stew must be seasoned way before you're going to cook them – refrigerated overnight in a marinade is best. However, the temperature slows down the marination time, so if you're in a rush and forgot to marinate your meat, leave it out to marinate for up to 2 hours as the meat will marinate quicker.

In fish and vegetables, the water content is a lot higher and they're able to absorb salt more quickly. I tend to use a 10 per cent cold brine (100g/3½oz of salt per 1 litre /1¾ pints of water) for fish for just 20 minutes. This firms up the fish and seasons it all the way through. You must dry it out fully between cloths before cooking, otherwise it'll likely stick to your frying pan. The same is true for aubergine. Ever wondered why its bitter flavour is removed when you brine the

aubergine in salt for 30 minutes before cooking? The salt balances bitter flavour more than sugar and seasons the aubergine.

When you season meat and vegetables, the fibres within are denatured and the cellulose in the plant cells breaks down, gelling the collagen and pectins and helping the tissue get super tender, i.e. the plant cells and meat proteins break down and get softer when marinated in salt.

You might have heard the term 'salt like the sea'. This refers to a blanching pot for vegetables or pasta or noodles. Blanching vegetables in water that tastes like the sea means that the water is at a higher concentration of salt than the vegetables, so the vegetables take in some of that salt. Don't be alarmed by the handfuls of salt you're adding to a pot as most of this will be heading down the drain.

Salt also helps strengthen gluten. I learned this the hard way after many failed attempts in trying to make hand-pulled noodles for MasterChef. They're super hard to make. The salt, protein content and alkalinity all help the gluten strengthen, which is why in the noodle recipe, Smoking Hot Noods (p. 96), I use a higher salt ratio, high-protein flour and add bicarbonate of soda, which increases the alkalinity. For hand-stretched noodles, there's more of an art to this and people study for years to get the technique just right. Medium-gluten flour is used and a salt solution and kan sui (an alkaline solution) is added to strengthen the gluten, with a series of stretch and folds to align the gluten strands. It's amazing to watch how hand-pulled noodles are made. Search for a video to be wowed; I'm not there yet but I love them and keep trying.

Salt is a key ingredient in all fermented foods; it keeps the environment sterile and prevents unwanted bacteria forming. It helps the veggies retain a crunch and slows the fermentation process to allow the lactic bacteria to develop a full flavour. A salt brine of 1.5–5 per cent is normally used when fermenting foods. To test out some fermented recipes, see the Funky Chilli Sauce (p. 249) or How I Kimchi (p. 162).

Salt doesn't just come in that white crystalline form; many umami ingredients such as miso and soy are also salty. So sometimes when you're tasting you might decide the dish doesn't need more salt, but you could use a little more miso or soy sauce to elevate the flavour. Everyone has different salt tolerances, so if needed you always have the salt shaker at the table to season to every-one's palate; however, the amount of salt needed to season at the table will be more than if you were to layer it in your cooking as it sits on top of the dish rather than having time to dissolve into the cells of the food. Just remember: however much you salt, it's going to be less than they use in restaurants. If someone in your family likes particularly salty food, test out a family experiment and serve their food on a blue plate. There have been studies that have shown that food eaten on a blue plate tastes saltier than on a white or any other colour plate!

# No waste

I hate it when you have that ingredient sitting at the back of the pantry and you don't know what to use it for. Please, if you do have a tub of gochujang left over, this should give you a little creative inspo to check out some of the other gochu recipes.

## KIDDISH

**Mirin:** Ponzu (p. 253), Shoyu Tare (p. 255), Miso and Gochu Marinated Cod (p. 234)

**Hoisin sauce**: Hong Kong-Style Pork Belly (p. 67), Cuddly Dan Dan Noods (p. 136)

**Sticky Soy Glaze:** Shitake Okonomiyaki (p. 232), Egg and Bacon Nasi Goreng (p.139)

**Brown sugar/palm sugar:** Brown Butter, Biscoff and Miso Blondies (p. 76), Vietnamese-Inspired Caramelised Pork Bowls (p. 106), Short Rib Rendang with Beef Dripping Crispy Potatoes (p. 148)

**Honey/maple syrup**: Peshwari Crust Cauli Korma (p. 54), Gochujang Spatchcock Chicken and Duck Fat Spicy Roasties (p. 103), Satay Prawns (p. 132)

## SPICE MASTER

**Funky chilli sauce/sriracha:** Sticky Sriracha Salmon (p. 62), Spicy Green Fish Cakes (p. 204), Mango and Thai Basil Pulled Chicken Flatbreads (p.211)

**Sichuan peppercorns:** Sichuan Fragrant Aubergine Tenders (p. 94), Sichuan Lamb Chops with Chilli Oil Crispy Potatoes (p. 108), Smacked Sichuan Pepper and Black Vinegar Cucumber (p. 165)

**Chilli oil:** Red Pepper and Kimchi Rigatoni (p. 135), Smoky Hispi Cabbage with Chilli Oil (p. 195), Fennel and Cucumber Slaw (p. 196)

**Gochujang:** Tteok-Bokki (p. 82), Korean No-Knead Focaccia (p. 100), Forbidden Black Garlic Rice (p. 242)

**Doubanjiang:** Beetroot Lentil Mapo Tofu (p. 86), Sichuan Fragrant Aubergine Tenders (p. 94)

## COMFORT

**Tahini:** Maple and Sesame Glazed Carrots (p. 58), Tuna Tataki with Gomae Dressing (p. 174), Charred Broccoli, Balsamic Red Onions and Tahini Soy Sauce (p. 199)

**Peanut butter:** No-Cook Satay Sauce (p. 252), Lu Rou Fan (p. 238)

**Coconut milk:** The Secret Katsu Dunkers (p. 144), Sea Bass Filipino-Inspired Kinilaw (p. 173), Coriander and Coconut Chicken Curry (p. 208)

**Noodles:** Bun Thit Nuong (p. 70), Smoking Hot Noods (p. 96), Khao Soi (p. 147)

**Japanese Mayo:** Korean Fried Chicken Burger (p. 64), Spicy Green Fish Cakes (p. 204), Soy-Glazed King Oyster Mushroom 'Murger' Pitas (p.226)

## TARTY

**Sake:** Chicken Yakitori with Togarashi Spice (p. 222), Shoyu Tare (p. 255), Miso and Shitake Mushroom Ramen (p.236)

**Tamarind:** Tamarind and Lime Glazed Salmon (p. 176), Goan-Inspired Prawn and Crab Curry with Blistered Tomatoes (p. 180), Green Coconut Chutney (p. 254)

**Shaoxing wine:** Black Pepper Portobello, Charred Peppers and Watercress Salad (p. 90), Cantonese-Style Steamed Fish (p. 202),

**Lemongrass:** Bun Thit Nuong (p. 70), Green Curry Mussels (p. 206)

**Kimchi:** Tteok-Bokki (p. 82), Red Pepper and Kimchi Rigatoni (p. 134)

## REFINED

**Coriander:** Aubergine Vindaloo (p. 92), Black Bean Makhani (p. 121), Gunpowder Pots (p. 168)

**Parsley:** Maple and Sesame Glazed Carrots (p. 58), Citrus Marinated Tomatoes with Garlicky Oil and Crispy Chapatis (p. 166), Cheesy Miso XO Corn (p. 230)

**Mint:** Tamarind and Lime Glazed Salmon (p. 176), Pork Larb (p. 214)

**Thai basil:** Mango and Thai Basil Pulled Chicken Flatbreads (p. 210), Thai Basil Beef Steaks (p. 212)

**Nam Jim:** Crispy Tofu Nuggz and Nam Jim (p. 170), Spicy Green Fish Cakes (p. 204)

## DARK HORSE

**Miso:** Miso Honey Slow-Roast Celeriac and Cavolo Nero (p. 56), Brown Butter, Biscoff and Miso Blondies (p. 76), Miso Sticky Toffee Pudding (p. 244)

**MSG:** Korean Fried Chicken Burger (p. 64), Fish Sauce Chicken Wings (p. 228)

**Dried shitake mushrooms:** Pickled Shrooms (p. 158), Miso and Shitake Mushroom Ramen (p. 236), Cheat XO Sauce (p. 255)

**Fish sauce:** Vietnamese-Inspired Caramelised Pork Bowls (p. 107), Fish Sauce Chicken Wings (p. 228)

**Dark soy sauce:** Black Pepper Portobello, Charred Peppers and Watercress Salad (p. 90), Lu Rou Fan (p. 238), Sticky Soy Glaze (p. 248)

# Cook's notes

### For best results
Read the ingredients list and do your choppy choppy before you start cooking.

**V/Ve** – V is veggie and Ve is vegan; however, there are swaps throughout the book and a lot of the meaty recipes can be adjusted to veggie alternatives.

### Serves
I've given approximate servings, but if you're not a big eater or you get really hungry (like our household) after running around you can scale up or down the recipes. Just remember to taste and adjust the cooking times.

### Tablespoons and teaspoons
Use the measuring type spoons, levelled not heaped unless stated. 1 tsp = 5ml and 1 tbsp = 15ml. However, if you want to use normal eating spoons these are approximately half a measuring spoon volume so double up the number of eating tablespoons.

### Herbage
All herbs are fresh, I don't often use dried. Always use flat leaf parsley, never curly.

### Salt
Use fine table salt unless flaky sea salt is specified when finishing a dish.

### Black pepper
This is freshly cracked, never ground.

### Sugar
Use white unless stated.

### Soy sauce
Use light unless dark is stated. Can be swapped for tamari.

### Kaffir lime leaves and curry leaves
Use fresh or frozen, not dried.

### Oils
Olive oil is extra virgin. Neutral oil is sunflower or vegetable (rapeseed or canola).

### Dairy
Yoghurt and crème fraîche are full-fat and plain and can be replaced with non-dairy alternatives. Cream is double cream 48% fat equivalent. Milk is always whole.

### Butter

I normally use unsalted but if you only have salted just use less salt in the recipe and taste as you go. Try not to use spreadable marge; it's not great on flavour.

### Eggs

These are medium unless stated and I normally use free-range (I love Burford Browns).

### Garlic, ginger, shallots and onions

Always use peeled. 'Minced' garlic and ginger means grated with a microplane or blended or crushed with the blade of a knife.

### Tamarind

I use paste as it's easier to find; however, they vary widely in concentration. If using concentrate please use half the required quantity, and if in doubt add a little and taste and repeat until you reach the desired flavour.

### Fresh chillies

Use with seeds, although you can remove the seeds and pith if you want less spice. Chillies are standard red chillies unless specified.

### Veggies

Use normal medium-sized veggies unless stated.

### Oven and hob temps

I have developed all the dishes using a standard fan oven and induction hob. You know your oven better than me so if you know it runs hotter or it has hot spots, use your Taste Kitchen instinct to taste, look, smell, see, hear and feel if a dish is ready rather than relying on timings. I also like to use a temperature probe to test if a dish is ready as this is most accurate.

### Weights

I like to use a digital read scale for measuring ingredients; it's more accurate and you can weigh straight into the bowl which means less washing-up.

# KIDDISH

I love sweet and sugar in all forms: I am fully addicted. With sweetness comes balance and you will learn how to use sweet ingredients in the perfect way to make your food super delicious.

Sweetness comes from carbohydrates and is one of the five basic tastes. Your tongue receptors sense the sweet carbs and tell your brain you're in for a sugar high. Detecting sweetness is one of the first things we learn about flavour as children. Newborns prefer high-sugar liquids that are sweeter than lactose, which is found in breast milk. We developed our love of sweetness because sweet flavours generally told our prehistoric ancestors that the food was safe to eat and energy-dense.

Studies have shown that we have sweet taste receptors in our tongue, but also in the lining of the gastrointestinal (GI) tract, as well as in our nose micro hairs and pancreatic cells. The GI tract sweet taste receptors control whether you're feeling hungry – or hangry – and the threshold of sweetness perception varies on the time of the day. I'll be the first to admit I am fully addicted to sugar and reach for the sweeties at approximately 4pm daily, literally eating a spoon of Nutella spread with zero regrets.

## MOOD AND ATMOSPHERE CAN ALSO AFFECT THE TASTE OF A DISH; HIGH-PITCHED MUSIC IS GENERALLY ASSOCIATED WITH SWEET FOOD, WHILE LOW-PITCHED, DEEP MUSIC IS PAIRED WITH RICH INTENSE FLAVOURS.

Sweetness is the least complex flavour; the more sweet ingredients you add, the sweeter a dish will be. However, sweetness can also be affected by acid. Have you ever made a raspberry sauce and cooked the fruit down in sugar and then at the very last minute added a squeeze of lemon? Yes, the sugar paired with the raspberries is delicious; however, once you add the lemon juice, it lifts more fruity flavours from the sauce.

Professor Charles Spence researches the psychology of eating. One of his studies looked at the link between our perception of taste and colour. He found that we perceive food as 10 per cent sweeter and 15 per cent more flavourful when eaten on a round, white plate, compared to an angular dark plate. Thanks to science, you can now ditch that trio of puds on that noughties slate. People generally eat less from a red plate as it could be seen as a danger and warning – good to know if you're on a diet. Mood and atmosphere can also affect the taste of a dish; high-pitched music is generally associated with sweet food, while low-pitched, deep music is paired with rich intense flavours.

Foods that are red and pink are generally associated with sweetness, possibly because we can recognise what we have previously tasted. For example, you see a strawberry and you know it's sweet. When I first visited Hong Kong, I visited these amazing markets filled with fruits and vegetables I had never seen before. I went to one fruit stand where they had a berry that looked like a cross between a blackberry and raspberry, but bigger and rounder. I later found out this fruit was a yumberry. I had no idea what it tasted like, but time was short and I was hosting a dinner that evening so I grabbed a bunch. Luckily, I could trust my instinct and the fruit was deliciously sweet, although nothing like a raspberry or blackberry.

There are many more sugars than just your standard granulated sugar. In professional kitchens, fructose is often used instead of sugar in fruity desserts because it brings out the fruity flavours. Throughout Asia all kinds of different sugars can be found: palm sugar in Indonesia, rock sugar in Hong Kong and jaggery in India. Although sweet flavours are delicious, we need to balance them with acidity, bitterness and spice. Sweetness comes in many different forms: in the following recipes I'll show you how to use it effectively and balance it.

## Kiddish ingredients

- Honey
- Palm sugar
- Brown sugar
- Sugar snap peas
- Maple syrup
- Rock sugar
- Mirin
- Strawberries
- White sugar
- Jaggery
- Cherry tomatoes
- Carrots

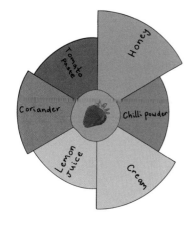

# Peshwari Crust Cauli Korma

As a child, my order from the local curry house had to be a Peshwari naan and chicken korma (yes, I was basic from birth). I'm taking that super sweet Peshwari spice mix we all love and roasting it into a crust for the cauliflower, then making a simple korma sauce. This is a great one to help introduce children to veggies.

SERVES 4

**Essential Equipment**
Heavy-based frying pan; stick blender

2 medium cauliflowers, leaves
    trimmed, sliced into 4 steaks
2 tbsp/30g/1oz butter, ghee or
    coconut oil
Sprinkle of salt
1 tbsp honey or maple syrup,
    plus extra for drizzling
2 tbsp/30g/1oz flaked almonds
2 tbsp desiccated coconut
Handful of chopped coriander,
    to garnish

FOR THE SAUCE
3 tbsp/45g/1½oz butter, ghee
    or coconut oil
1 medium onion, diced
1 tsp salt
2.5cm/1in piece of ginger,
    minced
2 garlic cloves, minced
1 cinnamon stick or
    ½ tsp ground cinnamon
3 cardamon pods, crushed
    with the blade of a knife
1 tsp ground coriander
½ tsp ground turmeric
½ tsp chilli powder
2 tsp tomato paste

**1.** Preheat the oven to 180°C (160°C fan oven) Gas 4.

**2.** Heat the butter, ghee or oil in a large frying pan and sear the cauliflower steaks with a sprinkle of salt in batches of two, caramelising on both sides. Transfer to an oven tray. Add any cauliflower trimmings and caramelise – if the pan looks dry, add a splash of oil – then add these to the tray, making sure not to overcrowd the tray, and roast for 30 minutes or until fully softened.

**3.** Make the sauce by melting the butter in a saucepan over a medium heat. Add the onion and salt and cook for 5 minutes until just colouring.

**4.** Throw in the ginger, garlic, cinnamon stick and cardamom pods and cook for 2–3 minutes until just fragrant.

———

100ml/3½fl oz double cream
    or plant-based cream
2 tsp sugar
Squeeze of lemon juice

**5.** Add the ground coriander, turmeric, chilli powder, tomato paste, double cream and 250ml/9fl oz water and cook down for 10 minutes.

**6.** Fish out the cinnamon stick and cardamom pods and blend the sauce with a stick blender until smooth, then throw back in the cinnamon stick and cardamom. Finish with the sugar and a squeeze of lemon juice, and **taste adjust** to your liking. Keep over a low heat until you're ready to serve.

**7.** Remove the cauliflower steaks from the oven and drizzle with honey. Sprinkle over the flaked almonds and desiccated coconut. Place back in the oven for a further 10 minutes until golden.

**8.** Serve the sauce on the plate and gently spread it into a circle with the back of your spoon. Add the cauliflower on top, finish with a drizzle of honey and garnish with chopped coriander.

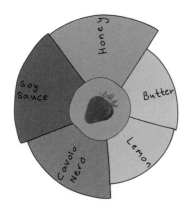

# Miso Honey Slow-Roast Celeriac and Cavolo Nero Ⓥ

**If you love a fondant potato, you'll love this buttery celeriac that's perfect for a winter's day. Cosy on up with a mug of mulled wine and a fire after a long walk. If you want to make the celeriac beforehand, simply cover with foil then reheat the celeriac with the cavolo nero and warm through the beans when you're ready to serve.**

SERVES 4 AS A SIDE OR
2 AS A MAIN

**Essential Equipment**
Large heavy ovenproof frying pan or high-sided oven tray

2 tbsp/30g/1oz butter or
    coconut oil
1 celeriac, peeled and quartered
Pinch of salt
1 tbsp white miso
4 tbsp honey or maple syrup
3 tbsp soy sauce
200ml/7fl oz veg stock or water
125g/4½oz cavolo nero or kale,
    de-stemmed and thinly sliced
220g/7½oz cooked butter beans
    (tinned)
Juice of 1 lemon

**1.** Preheat the oven to 200°C (180°C fan oven) Gas 6.

**2.** Melt the butter in a frying pan and add the celeriac quarters. Sprinkle with salt and caramelise the cut sides until a deep brown colour, about 10 minutes over a medium heat.

**3.** In a bowl whisk together the miso, honey, soy sauce and veg stock.

**4.** If your frying pan is oven-safe, flip the celeriac cut side up and then pour in the mixed stock around the celeriac. If your pans are not oven-safe place the celeriac on an oven tray, caramelised side up, and pour the stock around it. You want the liquid to come about three-quarters of the way up the celeriac. Cover with foil and place in the oven for 30–40 minutes.

**5.** Using an oven glove, remove the pan from the oven and check the celeriac is tender using a meat probe or wooden skewer. The liquid should be almost evaporated.

**6.** Add the cavolo nero and drained beans around the edges of the celeriac, re-cover with foil and cook for a further 10 minutes.

**7.** Remove and squeeze over the lemon juice. Taste a little of the cavolo nero and remaining liquid and **taste adjust**, then serve.

# Maple and Sesame Glazed Carrots ⓥ

Level up your Sunday roast with these sticky sesame carrots. As the carrots roast, the glaze will become gooey and the sesame seeds stick to the carrot like brittle. Perfectly paired with a quick tahini sauce.

SERVES 4 AS A SIDE

**Essential Equipment**
Oven tray; mini-whisk

1 tbsp/15g/½oz butter or
   coconut oil
½ tbsp miso
3 tbsp maple syrup or honey
300g/10½oz baby carrots,
   scrubbed, or normal carrots,
   peeled and sliced
1 tsp sesame seeds
2 tbsp tahini
1 tbsp lemon juice
Handful of parsley, chopped

**1.** Preheat the oven to 200°C (180°C fan oven) Gas 6.

**2.** In a small saucepan or microwave melt the butter and whisk together with the miso, maple syrup and 2 tablespoons water.

**3.** Add the carrots to a lined oven tray and pour over the sweet melted butter mix. Roast for 30–35 minutes.

**4.** Remove and sprinkle over the sesame seeds, then roast for a further 5 minutes.

**5.** In a small bowl using a mini-whisk, mix together the tahini and lemon juice until it looks like sand. Slowly add in ½ tablespoon of cold water at a time until the mixture reaches double cream consistency, 1–2 tablespoons in total.

**6.** Remove the carrots from the oven and check they are tender and caramelised. Add the carrots to a plate, finish with a sprinkle of chopped parsley and serve with the tahini sauce.

**7.** Sneak a little bite and **taste adjust** (squeeze a little more lemon juice over the carrots if it's too rich or mix in some miso to the tahini sauce if you want more umami flavour).

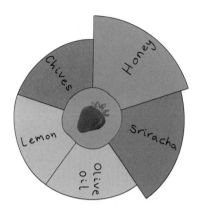

# Halloumi and Baked Cherry Toms with Hot Honey Drizzle Ⓥ

**This is 100% yummy and super versatile. Serve it for lunch, as a starter with crusty bread or for brunch with poachies: think about halloumi shakshuka with a mimosa ...**

SERVES 4 AS A STARTER OR SIDE, OR 2 FOR BRUNCH

**Essential Equipment**
Potato masher or large fork

215g/7½oz halloumi, diced
2 tbsp olive oil
20–30 cherry tomatoes
Pinch of salt
2 garlic cloves, minced
1 batch Sriracha Hot Honey
(p. 248)
Squeeze of lemon juice
Chopped chives or any herbage

TO SERVE
My Mum's Chapatis (p. 116) or
flatbreads for mopping

**1.** Place a frying pan over a medium heat and add 1 table-spoon of the olive oil and the halloumi. Caramelise on all sides until golden brown, then remove from the pan and reserve on the side.

**2.** Turn up the heat and add the remaining olive oil and the cherry tomatoes with a pinch of salt. Make sure to blister the tomatoes and cook for about 5–10 minutes.

**3.** When the tomatoes start to shrivel and pop, turn down the heat to medium and start to smash them gently with a potato masher or large fork. Add in the garlic and cook for a further 10 minutes.

**4.** Meanwhile, make the Sriracha Hot Honey (p. 248).

**5.** Stir the golden halloumi and lemon juice through the tomatoes and allow to heat for 2 minutes before serving, drizzling over the Sriracha Hot Honey and sprinkling with chives.

**6. Taste adjust** just before serving – taste a little and make sure there's enough acidity to cut through the rich halloumi.

**7.** Serve with some chapatis, flatbreads or crusty bread for mopping the sauce up.

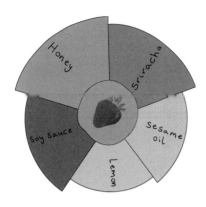

# Sticky Sriracha Salmon

SERVES 4

**Essential Equipment**
Oven tray; grill or blow torch

2 tbsp honey
1 tbsp soy sauce
½ tbsp sesame oil
1 tsp garlic powder
2 tbsp sriracha
800g/1lb 12oz side of salmon or
    4 x 200g/7oz salmon fillets
1 lemon, zested and wedged

**If you're looking for a super speedy dinner, this recipe won't disappoint.**

**1.** Combine the honey, soy sauce, sesame oil, garlic powder and sriracha to make a marinade, then **taste adjust**.

**2.** Marinate the fish and leave for 20 minutes.

**3.** Preheat the oven to 220°C (200°C fan oven) Gas 7.

**4.** Remove the salmon from the marinade and drain slightly but do not wipe. Then place the salmon on a lined oven tray, skin side down. Reserve the rest of the marinade.

**5.** Bake for 12–15 minutes for a half side or 10–12 minutes for fillets. Paint over the marinade at 5-minute intervals until the fish is super glazed.

**6.** After the time is up or when the fish reaches 45–50°C internal temperature, remove the fish from the oven. If you want a little extra char pop the fish under the grill or use a blow torch to lightly char the surface. (If you're using baking parchment, be careful that it doesn't burn.)

**7.** Grate over some lemon zest and serve with wedges of lemon.

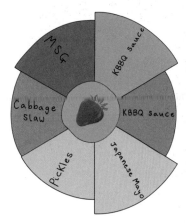

# Korean Fried Chicken Burger

There's nothing quite like fried chicken. I mean, I made it twice on *MasterChef*. I ended up reading scientific papers on how different ingredients affect the tenderness of the chicken. There are various natural enzymes (papain and bromelain) from pineapple, kiwi and pear that tenderise the meat. This is why you see pineapple and pear often used in different marinades. Here I'm using pickle juice, which is also a great tenderiser and gives it a super delish sour flavour, as well as buttermilk and MSG to get the ultimate tender juicy chicken. If you wanted to have a few sharers, then you could always cut the thighs down into nuggz, whip up some popcorn chicken and drench them in Buttery KBBQ sauce (p. 248).

SERVES 4

**Essential Equipment**
Serrated knife; wok or cast-iron frying pan; tongs

240ml/8½fl oz buttermilk
½ tsp salt
1 tbsp pickle juice
1 tsp MSG (optional)
4 chicken thigh fillets

FOR THE BREADER
50g/1½oz cornflour
200g/7oz plain flour
1 tsp paprika
1 tsp garlic powder
½ tsp salt
50g/1½oz cornflakes (optional)
300–600ml/11–19fl oz oil
   for frying

FOR THE SLAW
½ white cabbage, thinly sliced
   (I prefer to use a mandoline)
2 tbsp pickle juice
Handful of dill, chopped
1 tbsp fish sauce
1 tbsp brown sugar

TO SERVE
4 Brioche burger buns, sliced
   in half
2 tbsp softened butter
1 batch Japanese Mayo (p. 251)
   or Kewpie mayo

1 batch Buttery Korean BBQ
   Sauce (p. 248)
Gherkins or Quick Pickled Cucs
   (p. 161), sliced

**1.** Whisk the buttermilk, salt, pickle juice and MSG in a container.

**2.** Add the thighs, cover and marinate in the fridge for at least 6 hours but preferably overnight.

**3.** Have the Japanese mayo and Korean BBQ sauce ready before beginning the recipe.

**4.** Mix the cabbage with the pickle juice, dill, fish sauce and brown sugar. Scrunch up the cabbage and dressing with your hands. Let the slaw sit for 30 minutes.

**5.** Carefully heat enough oil for deep-frying in a large wok or saucepan to 170°C, making sure not to fill it any higher than halfway. Place an oven tray with a drying rack or kitchen paper on it nearby.

**6.** Take the chicken out of the fridge. Mix together the cornflour, flour, spices and salt and, using your hands, crush in the cornflakes, if using. Mix in a couple of tablespoons of the buttermilk chicken marinade and smush it together to get a few crumbly bits.

**7.** When the oil is hot coat one chicken thigh in the breader, really pushing the flour mix into the chicken, then dust off the excess flour. Gently place the chicken in the oil away from you, so that the oil doesn't splash back at you.

→

**8.** Fry one or two thighs at a time for 5–7 minutes or until the internal temperature is above 80–90°C. Make sure the oil temperature doesn't drop below 140°C and keep the chicken moving gently in the oil. Remove with tongs and drain on the resting tray. Repeat with the remaining chicken.

**9.** Butter the brioche buns on the cut side. Heat a large frying pan and toast until golden brown.

**10.** Build the burger: spread mayo on each piece of brioche, then add slaw, the chicken and ladle on the KBBQ sauce. Top off with gherkins and the other slice of brioche.

**11. Taste and adjust** after your first bite. More Buttery Korean BBQ Sauce adds more sweetness; add pickles if it's too rich.

**Notes**

Don't be alarmed if the chicken is pink: if you probed the temperature to over 80°C it's **very** cooked. This is the buttermilk retaining moisture.

The aim is to get a textured surface on the chicken before cooking, the rougher the surface on the chicken the crispier the end result.

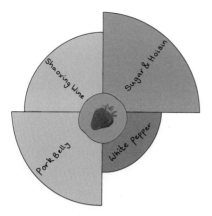

# *Fancy* Hong Kong-Style Pork Belly

In Hong Kong there are loads of roast meat restaurants hanging delicious goose, char siu and, of course, crispy pork belly, or siu yuk. These restaurants have huge ovens to cook the meat until the skin is deliciously crisp. We're going to do a home work-around that I have found to give the most consistent puffy skin. It's like a pork scratching on top of a juicy pork belly. Traditionally siu yuk is served with saucers of watered-down mustard and sugar. I'm serving it with a hoisin-based dipping sauce.

SERVES 4–6

### Essential Equipment
Heatproof ladle; resting rack; high-sided oven tray

1kg/2lb 3oz pork belly, bones removed but skin intact (preferably from a reputable butcher)
1 tsp five-spice powder
½ tsp white pepper
1 tsp salt
500ml/18fl oz vegetable oil

FOR THE DIPPING SAUCE
½ tsp salt
3 tbsp Shaoxing rice wine
2 tbsp white sugar
½ tsp five-spice powder
3 tbsp hoisin sauce
¼ tsp white pepper

MAKE PUFFY JUICY PORK BELLY

**1.** Choose good quality pork belly from the middle part of the pig; you want a nice layer of fat. Ask your butcher to help you select it.

**2.** Using the tip of a paring knife, lightly score the skin, making sure not to go down too deep into the fat or the meat. Use a fine metal pokey stick or fork to gently poke loads of holes in the top surface of the pork skin, about ¼cm deep. Again, don't go too deep into the fat, otherwise the fat will run up and the skin won't puff.

**3.** Mix together the five-spice, pepper and half the salt. Flip the pork over and rub the marinade over the meat, making sure not to touch the skin. Flip the pork back over and sprinkle the rest of the salt on the skin. Allow to sit for 20 minutes, after which time you will notice water

appear. Wipe away any water and then place the pork on top of a metal rack in a foil-lined high-sided oven tray so that air can circulate all around the pork and the skin really dries out. Leave the pork in the fridge for 18–48 hours.

**4.** Preheat the oven to 160°C (140°C fan oven) Gas 3.

**5.** Transfer the pork in the tray to the oven and cook for for 3–4 hours. You want the internal temperature of the pork to reach 91°C.

**6.** Remove the pork and allow to rest on a trivet for 15–20 minutes while you heat the oil in a large pot or wok to 200–210°C.
**Warning: BE SUPER CAREFUL!** Don't step away from the pot, I don't want you burning yourself or starting any house fires.

**7.** Ladle the oil over the pork and allow it to puff up. Keep ladling hot oil until all the skin becomes white and puffy.

**8.** Mix all the dipping sauce ingredients together and **taste adjust**. You want the sweetness and sharpness to cut through the rich belly.

**9.** Slice the pork against the grain into squares – I like to use a long serrated knife – and serve with the dipping sauce.

**Note**
If you have a gas hob, I would suggest you don't pour oil over an open flame; instead, after the pork is done cooking in the oven turn on your grill. Set the pork on the lowest shelf of your oven and grill the pork, keeping an eye on it as it will caramelise and burn easily. If any part is catching, remove and cover the area with foil before placing back under the grill until all the pork is crisp.

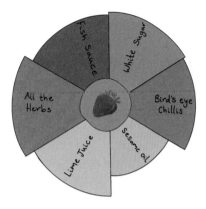

# Bun Thit Nuong (Vietnamese-Style Grilled Pork and Noodles)

Bun thit nuong is one of my favourite Vietnamese dishes. It literally means grilled pork and noodles. You might think it's simple in flavour from the title, but there's loads going on. I fell in love with it in Ho Chi Minh: there was this one street with a lady fanning her barbecue and filling the street with a delicious, smoky pork aroma. I sat down on a rickety plastic chair and enjoyed this amazing bowl of noodles. Sweet, sour and charred caramelised pork with loads of aromatic herby flavours all in one bowl.

SERVES 4

### Essential Equipment
Tiny blender; mandoline or Y-shaped peeler

FOR THE PORK
700g/1lb 8oz pork shoulder
  or 4 x 175g/6oz pork shoulder
  steaks
4 spring onions, sliced, white
  and green parts separated
1 garlic clove, minced
2 tbsp white sugar
2 tbsp fish sauce
2 tbsp soy sauce
2 tbsp sesame oil
2 lemongrass sticks, smashed
  to split open

FOR THE BOWL
1 batch Nuoc Cham (p. 253)
2 carrots, sliced into ribbons
2 tbsp rice vinegar or white
  wine vinegar
4 spring rolls, shop-bought
  (optional)
600g/1lb 5oz vermicelli rice
  noodles
100g/3½oz salad leaves
  (preferably butter lettuce)
½ cucumber, super thinly sliced
Handful of mint, picked
Handful of coriander, picked
Handful of Thai basil or normal
  basil, picked

**1.** Place the pork steaks between two sheets of baking parchment or cling film and smash them with the flat side of a meat tenderiser or rolling pin until just 5mm/¼ inch thick.

**2.** Blend the white part of the spring onion (keeping the green part for the garnish), garlic, sugar, fish sauce, soy sauce and sesame oil, then add lemongrass. Use the mixture to marinate the pork for at least 2 hours but preferably overnight, in the fridge, covered.

**3.** Preheat the oven to 200°C (180°C fan oven) Gas 6.

**4.** Make the Nuoc Cham dipping sauce (p. 253).

**5.** Dress the sliced carrots with rice vinegar.

**6.** If using spring rolls, heat them according to their cooking instructions.

**7.** Prepare the noodles according to their cooking instructions: normally you pour boiling water over the noodles and allow to soften for 10 minutes in a bowl.

**8.** Remove the pork from the marinade and pat dry. Heat a frying pan over a medium-high heat with a splash of cooking oil and cook the pork steaks one or two at a time; do not overcrowd the pan. Cook for 2 minutes on each side for a caramel colour then remove and place on a lined oven tray. Repeat with the other steaks. Put the steaks into the oven to cook for a further 5–10 minutes until golden brown and tender. Then remove and allow the steaks to rest on a chopping board.

**9.** Add the softened and drained noods to the bowl, and top one side with fresh salad, carrots and cucumber. Slice the rested pork against the grain and layer over the noodles. Pour over half the Nuoc Cham and garnish with the herbs and the green spring onion parts.

**10.** Serve with the rest of the Nuoc Cham dipping sauce and hot spring rolls at the table and enjoy. **Taste and adjust** your individual bowl as you eat.

**Note**
This pork is *great* on the barbecue. To cook, heat charcoal on one side of the barbecue. Cook over direct heat to get a great crust, but be careful of any flames. Then move the meat to the other side, away from the coal for indirect cooking. Cover and cook for 5–10 minutes.

# Japanese Cheesecake

I feel like everyone has become obsessed with the super fudgy, gooey Basque cheesecake. That's all great, but I also love light, fluffy Japanese-style cheesecake, which has an almost squishy, cloud-like texture. I'm topping mine with Chantilly cream and strawberries as one of the iconic 7/11 Japanese sandwiches is strawberries and cream.

MAKES 1 LARGE CAKE FOR 6–8

**Essential Equipment**
20cm/8in diameter, 8–10cm/ 3–4in tall cake tin; stand mixer; large high-sided oven tray

240g/8½oz cream cheese
40g/1½oz unsalted butter, plus extra for greasing
75ml/2½fl oz whole milk
Pinch of salt
1 vanilla pod, split and scraped
6 eggs
60g/2oz plain flour
½ tsp lemon juice
135g/4½oz caster sugar
100ml/3½fl oz double cream
2 tbsp icing sugar
Strawberries to decorate, or other in-season fruit

MAKE THE PERFECT BATTER

**1.** Preheat the oven to 180°C (160°C fan oven) Gas 4.

**2.** Butter the inside of your cake tin and line with baking parchment.

**3.** To a small saucepan add the cream cheese, butter, milk, salt and scraped vanilla seeds. Melt over a low heat and whisk together until there are no lumps.

**4.** Separate the egg yolks into a bowl and reserve the whites in a separate clean, dry stand mixer bowl.

**5.** Lightly whisk the egg yolks, then stir the melted cream cheese mix into the yolks.

**6.** Sift the flour into the mix and stir together.

**7.** To make the meringue, take the egg whites and add in the lemon juice. Whisk (an electric whisk is easier) so it's light and foamy. Gradually add in the caster sugar until the meringue is thick and glossy. (Using a stand mixer gets great results.)

**8.** Add a third of the meringue to the yolk mixture and whisk together, then fold in the rest of the meringue a third at a time and mix until there are no more white bits, but try not to overmix.

**9.** Fill the lined tin with cake mix up to 15mm/½in from the rim and place in a large, high-sided oven tray with a tea towel under the cake tin.

**10.** Fill the tray with hot water so it comes halfway up the cake tin. Put the tray in the oven.

**11.** Bake for 20 minutes. Open the oven and count for 5 seconds, then turn down the oven to 120°C (100°C fan oven) Gas ½ and bake for a further 60 minutes.

**12.** Turn off the oven and keep the door slightly open by placing a tea towel in the seal, creating a slight gap. Allow the cake to cool inside the oven for a further 20 minutes.

**13.** Remove the cake from the oven. Using an oven cloth to protect your hand from the heat, invert the cheesecake from the tin onto your hand. Then place the cheesecake onto a plate and allow to cool completely.

**14.** To make Chantilly cream to decorate the cake, add the double cream and icing sugar to a bowl and whip to stiff peaks.

**15.** Spread the Chantilly over the top of the cake and decorate with cut strawbs.

### Tip
This is a pastry recipe so we need to keep the cheesecake base consistent; however, you can get creative with toppings or add a little lemon zest to bring acidity.

### Notes
If there are any cracks in the surface simply cover them with the Chantilly cream. The cheesecake will decrease in size as you allow it to rest, just like a soufflé does. This is normal but don't worry, it'll be super fluffy on the inside.

I like to keep the used vanilla pod and add it to a 1:1 ratio of sugar and water, bring it to the boil and then store it in an airtight container to make a vanilla syrup.

# Brown Butter, Biscoff and Miso Blondies

Okay, I'll admit it, I'm basic. I love Biscoff. I love white chocolate. I love miso. I'm whacking it all together into more delicious things and it's all going to be spiced, salted caramel sweet yumminess.

MAKES 9 LARGE PIECES OR
18 BITE-SIZE PIECES

## Essential Equipment
23 x 33cm/9 x 13in baking tray

225g/8oz unsalted butter
250g/9oz light brown sugar
3 tbsp miso (preferably white)
2 whole eggs
1 egg yolk
285g/10oz plain flour
½ tsp baking powder
200g/7oz white chocolate chips
150g/5oz Biscoff spread
20 Biscoff biscuits

**1.** Preheat the oven to 200°C (180°C fan oven) Gas 6 and line the baking tray with baking parchment.

**2.** In a saucepan melt the butter and caramelise it until golden brown, then allow to cool for 10 minutes.

**3.** Whisk together the melted butter, sugar and miso in a large bowl making sure there are no lumps. Allow to cool slightly.

**4.** Add the egg and egg yolk, stirring until completely combined. Set aside.

**5.** Sift the plain flour into a separate bowl and mix in the cornflour and baking powder.

**6.** Gradually stir the dry ingredients into the wet until completely combined. Then fold in the white chocolate chips, reserving a handful.

**7.** Add half the mix to the lined tray and add 5 teaspoons of Biscoff spread. Break up half of the biscuits and scatter them over.

**8.** Add the rest of the blondie mix, then spoon on 5 more teaspoons of Biscoff spread and swirl the mix. Top with more broken-up biscuits and the rest of the white chocolate chips.

**9.** Bake for 25–35 minutes or until a toothpick inserted in the centre comes out clean with some sticky bits – you want the blondie gooey.

**10.** Remove the blondie from the oven and allow it to cool, then pop it in the fridge for 15–20 minutes and allow it to set.

## Note
I find it easiest to cut the blondie with a Victorinox pastry knife (bread knife).

## Tip
This is one recipe that is sweet and comforting loveliness. If you want any more sweetness drizzle on white chocolate at the end, but I wouldn't change the base too much. However, you could swap the Biscoff for peanut butter.

# SPICE MASTER

No spice fazes you. You enjoy eating a phall, lap up Sichuan hot pot, or chow down a Thai papaya salad and laugh in the face of others reaching for the cooling yoghurt or milk. You have a collection of chilli condiments in the pantry and are always looking to add a little extra heat to a dish, but let me share that spice is not a taste: it's a sensation.

Let's break this flavour down into three main factors: taste, olfactory sense and trigeminal sense.

◆ Taste is what your tongue picks up – sweet, sour, salty, bitter, savoury, and possibly fattiness.

◆ Olfactory senses are what the senses in your nose distinguish. A pear and an apple, for example, are sweet but have different aroma compounds.

◆ The trigeminal system detects pain, the sense when you feel a pan is burning hot.

Your trigeminal system controls spice sensation; the nerve endings in your tongue detect temperature, touch and pain. Spice is a reaction to the pain caused by capsaicin (the spice molecule). As the pain increases, your tongue numbs as a protective mechanism; although it's an irritant, the capsaicin is not harmful. There are mixed findings on whether you can desensitise your tongue nerve endings and effectively increase your spice pain tolerance, or if there is no link between increased exposure to spice and becoming a Spice Master. Another hypothesis is that **Spice Masters are sensation seekers, adrenaline junkies, gamblers and gregarious types.** Spice Masters can be benign masochists and enjoy negative sensations if they know no harm will come to them.

If you have accidentally gnawed down on a Carolina Reaper (the world's hottest chilli at 2,200,000 Scoville heat units), the pain can last up to 6 hours. At this point, your best option is casein, the protein found in dairy products, as it detaches capsaicin, the spice molecule, from the pain receptors. Another option is to add mint, which also uses the trigeminal system in the opposite way to the chilli heat and cools the sensitive nerves. It has the added benefit of giving you fresh breath.

Most people think that the seeds are the spicy part of the chilli. However, the spiciest part is the white tissue around the seeds, the chilli placenta.

Chilli peppers are indigenous to the Andes of western South America. Christopher Columbus brought chilli peppers back to the old world while seeking out a new trade route to Asia and looking for black peppercorns. He found the chilli pepper in Mexico and brought it back; however, the Portuguese were responsible for distributing it to Asia, where it was first adopted by chefs in India in the 1500s. At this point, the Indian chefs were used to cooking with spiced ingredients like black pepper, cinnamon and ginger. As the Portuguese empire grew, so did the spread of chillies, across to China and beyond.

I feel there are different types of spice: the slap-you-round-the-face, effing hot kind; the builders; and then there's Sichuan hotpot. Sichuan cooking is known for the use of Sichuan peppercorns. I do not claim to be a Spice Master, but I am fond of a little chilli heat. When I experienced my first hotpot in Chengdu, China, I wanted to try it how the locals were ordering. So I ordered the spiciest one on the menu, and was wondering why so many men in the restaurant had tucked up their t-shirts like they were in a Britney Spears video. I also noticed that there were little drawers built into the table with super absorbent paper napkins. The huge steaming soup came to the table boiling like a witch's cauldron, with a boatload of Chinese chillies and Sichuan peppercorns. I added the prepared ingredients and let the smells start to burn the inside of my nose. I'm not a quitter though; I had to have a taste. So when the soup was ready to taste I took a mouthful and I didn't think it was as spicy as it smelt; so far so good. So I eagerly started munching all the sausages, veggies and noodles. Then it hit me. My god! It was like a burning sensation coming up from my stomach in waves, I couldn't feel my tongue and I started sweating. This is where the napkins came in handy. Unfortunately no cold water was on offer; just hot tea. Sichuan hotpot is still one of my favourite meals and if you love spicy food it's a must!

I find that adding a little chilli kick to a dish can balance the sweetness, sourness or richness of a dish; it also adds another dimension. Different chillies are used throughout regions of Asia, from green rocket chillies and Kashmiri chilli powder in India to dried chillies and Sichuan peppercorns in Sichuan, gochujang in South Korea, and wasabi and togarashi in Japan. Chilli is well-loved throughout Asia, and together we'll explore some of these delicious dishes.

## Spice Master ingredients

- Fresh chillies
- Sichuan peppercorns
- Doubanjiang
- Mustard
- Rocket
- Dried chillies
- Chilli oil
- Togarashi
- Radish
- Ginger
- Sriracha
- Gochujang
- Wasabi
- Watercress

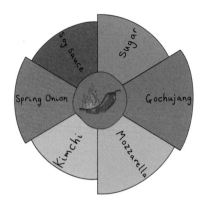

SERVES 4

**Essential Equipment**
Large, deep frying pan or wok

FOR THE RICE CAKES
500g/1lb 1½oz Korean rice cakes, shop bought
OR
300g/10½oz rice flour
135g/4½oz tapioca starch or cornflour
½ tsp salt
2 tsp sugar
300ml/11fl oz boiled water

FOR THE SAUCE
3 tbsp gochujang
1 tsp gochugaru (Korean chilli flakes) or chilli powder
1½ tbsp sugar
1½ tbsp soy sauce
3 garlic cloves, minced
100g/3½oz How I Kimchi (p. 162) or shop bought kimchi (optional)
100g/3½oz grated mozzarella cheese or plant-based, plus extra to serve
2 spring onions, finely sliced
Toasted sesame seeds

HOW TO ROLL RICE CAKES

# **Tteok-Bokki** (Korean-Inspired Spicy Cheesy Rice Cakes) Ⓥ

When the lights turn off in Seoul the street markets come alive with pojangmacha, street food tents that sell all sorts of delights. One of my faves is tteok-bokki. It's so well loved in Seoul that a whole street food market is dedicated to this one dish, Sindang-dong Tteok-bokki Town.

I see tteok-bokki as the poutine of South Korea – well, this cheesy version is at least. The rice cakes have a squishy texture almost like gnocchi, they're drenched in a super spicy, umami sauce and this version is covered in melted cheese for extra indulgence. If you want to lighten up this dish simply remove the cheese. You could also make the rice cakes ahead, or if you spot them in your local Asian specialist shop pick up a bag and you've got the quickest meal, best enjoyed with a beer.

**1.** If you are making your own rice cakes, mix the rice flour and starch with the salt and sugar. Gradually add in boiling water and mix until you have a firm dough. You may need a few tablespoons more water. Place the dough in a bowl and cover.

**2.** Take a quarter of the dough and roll it out to a long sausage shape about 1cm/½in in diameter. It can start to break as it rolls; if it does add ½ tablespoon of water to your hands and re-knead the dough.

**3.** Cut the dough into 3cm cylinders and place on a tray. Repeat with the remaining dough.

**4.** Heat a large, deep frying pan or wok of salted water until boiling.

**5.** Meanwhile, whisk the gochujang, gochugaru, sugar, soy sauce and garlic for the sauce together in a small bowl.

**6.** Boil the rice cakes for 2–3 minutes, then strain through a slotted spoon, leaving the rice cakes and a small amount of starchy water in the pan. Add in the kimchi and sauce and let everything come to the boil.

**7.** Cook over a low heat for 5–10 minutes until the sauce has thickened.

**8.** Turn down the heat and sprinkle the cheese over the rice cakes. Cover with a lid until all the cheese has fully melted. **Taste adjust** to your palate.

**9.** Take off the heat and sprinkle with more cheese, spring onions and sesame seeds.

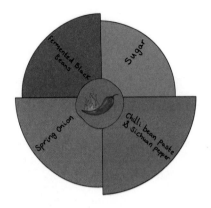

# Beetroot Lentil Mapo Tofu

Let me introduce you to Sichuan cooking, famous for its spicy, bold food, with loads of garlic, ginger and the mouth-numbing Sichuan pepper.

Mapo tofu is one of the most famous Chinese dishes, enjoyed all over the world. You may have had it with minced pork or beef. I feel that the beetroot and lentils are a great alternative and give this dish a unique earthy flavour.

**SERVES 4**

### Essential Equipment
Wok or large saucepan;
large spoon

500g/1lb 1½oz silken tofu, diced
4 tbsp neutral oil
1 tsp Sichuan peppercorns, ground, plus extra to serve
2½ tbsp Sichuan chilli broad bean paste (doubanjiang), or if you can't find it use gochujang
1 tbsp fermented black beans (optional)
2 spring onions, sliced
2 garlic cloves, minced
2.5cm/1in piece of ginger, minced
2 beetroots, peeled and cut into 1cm/½in dice (use gloves)
50g/1½oz puy or green lentils
600–800ml/20–27fl oz stock or water
2–4 tbsp Philli's Chilli Oil (p. 250) or Chinese chilli oil
1 tsp sugar
1 tbsp cornflour

TO SERVE
Steamed rice
Spring onion greens

**1.** Dice the tofu and cover in boiling water; this will firm it up.

**2.** You need to work quite quickly for the first stages so make sure you have all the veg prepped and ready.

**3.** Add the oil to your wok over a high heat, making sure it's super hot and seasoned. Add the ground Sichuan peppercorns and keep stirring for 10–20 seconds to make sure nothing catches.

**4.** Add the doubanjiang and allow the oil to become deep red in colour, about 2–3 minutes.

**5.** Add in the fermented black beans with the spring onions, garlic and ginger.

**6.** Finally add the beetroot, lentils and stock. Cover and allow everything to simmer. Cook over a medium heat for 25–30 minutes until the lentils are nearly soft. Top up the water if the pan ever looks dry.

**7.** Drain the tofu from the water and layer it gently on top of the beetroot lentil mix, spoon on the chilli oil and sugar, then top up with a little more water if required.

**8.** Cook on low for a further 10 minutes. Do not stir the pot initially as the tofu will firm up once braised.

**9.** Mix the cornflour with 2 tablespoons of cold water and add to the pan. Gently stir and wait for the sauce to fully thicken.

**10.** Serve with steamed rice and garnish with spring onion greens, and more Sichuan pepper if you dare.

### Taste adjust
If it's a little too spicy cool it down with another teaspoon of sugar.

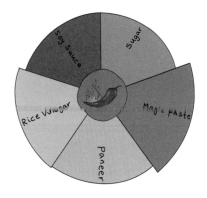

# Raging Chilli Paneer Puffs with Rocket Chilli and Lemon Yog (V)

I love Indochinese flavours. These chilli paneer puffs are *wow* – encased in a crispy pastry and served with a cool lemony yoghurt, it's the perfect starter. If you want to skip the samosa part and have the chilli paneer as a side or main, you will need to halve the cornflour in the recipe and add 240ml/8½fl oz water.

Let me introduce you to magic paste, invented by my friend, the Spice Queen, Ren Patel. Magic paste is a fusion of ginger and green chilli, and you can add it at the start, middle or end of your cooking, or even serve it on the table as a condiment. If you prefer a dish a little extra hot, just whack in a spoon of magic paste.

SERVES 4–6/MAKES 12 SAMOSAS

**Essential Equipment**
Small blender or stick blender, baking parchment

FOR THE MAGIC PASTE
20 green rocket chillies, roughly chopped
50g/1½oz ginger, roughly chopped
2–6 tbsp water

FOR THE PUFFS
3 tbsp neutral oil
225g/8oz paneer, cut into 1cm/½in dice
2 garlic cloves, minced
6 tbsp magic paste
2 spring onions, sliced
1 tbsp soy sauce
2 tbsp tomato ketchup
1 tbsp rice vinegar
1 tsp sugar
2 tbsp cornflour
2 sheets pre-rolled puff pastry
1 egg, beaten
Sprinkle of chilli flakes (optional)

FOR THE SPICED LEMONY YOG
150g/5oz plain full-fat yoghurt
Juice of ½ lemon
½ tsp garam masala
¼ tsp salt

**1.** To make the magic paste, blend the green chillies and ginger with just enough water to bind into a smooth paste.

**2.** Heat the oil in a pan over a medium–high heat and fry the paneer until golden brown.

**3.** Add in the garlic, magic paste and spring onion and fry for 2 minutes until it starts to smell aromatic. Add the soy sauce, tomato ketchup, rice vinegar and sugar.

**4.** Whisk together the cornflour and 4 tablespoons of cold water with a fork and then add this to the pan and allow the sauce to thicken. **Taste adjust** to your palate.

**5.** Transfer the filling to a shallow tray and let it come down to room temperature.

**6.** Preheat the oven to 200°C (180°C fan oven) Gas 6.

**7.** Remove the pastry from the fridge and unroll gently without cracking the pastry. Cut it into 10cm/4in squares; try to work quickly as the pastry is easier to handle when cold.

**8.** Add a heaped tablespoon of filling to each square, brush the edges with egg and fold over into a triangle.

**9.** Brush the outside of the pastry with egg, sprinkle over some chilli flakes and place on a lined baking tray. Bake for 18–20 minutes until glazed and golden.

**10.** Mix the lemony yoghurt ingredients together and serve with the pastries.

**Tip**
This recipe makes a big batch of magic paste, so freeze it in ice-cube trays and you're ready to go each time.

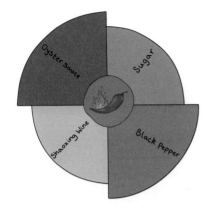

# Black Pepper Portobello, Charred Peppers and Watercress Salad

Who needs black pepper beef when you can have black pepper portobellos? It's super meaty and makes a great side or main and served with a peppery salad you can feel the warm weather. I love pressing the mushrooms between two frying pans, squeezing out the water makes the mushrooms super intense and firm.

SERVES 2 AS A MAIN OR
4 AS A SIDE

**Essential Equipment**
2 cast-iron or heavy-based frying pans, one slightly smaller than the other

2 tbsp neutral oil
4 large portobello mushrooms, stalks trimmed
1 red pepper, sliced
6 Thai shallots, peeled and halved, or 3 banana shallots, peeled and quartered
Pinch of salt
2 garlic cloves, minced
5cm/2in piece of ginger, minced
3 tbsp oyster sauce or
    1 tbsp dark soy sauce
2 tsp light soy sauce
1–3 tsp ground black pepper
¼ tsp sugar
2 tbsp Shaoxing wine or
    dry sherry
2 tsp cornflour

FOR THE SALAD
½ tbsp English mustard
1 tbsp sesame oil
1 tbsp rice vinegar
100g/3½oz watercress, washed
6 radishes, sliced

**1.** Heat the frying pan over a medium heat with the neutral oil.

**2.** Add the portobello mushrooms stalk side down, and the peppers and shallots cut side down. Season with a good pinch of salt. Add a second pan on top of the veg and let the weight of the pan gently press the vegetables during the cooking process. Cook the veg on one side for 12–15 minutes; you want to achieve a deep caramel crust. If it looks too dark, turn down the heat.

**3.** While the veg is cooking whisk together the garlic, ginger, oyster sauce, soy sauce, black pepper, sugar and Shaoxing wine.

**4.** Remove the second pan and check the vegetables. Once they reach a deep caramel colour, add the sauce and cook for 2 minutes.

**5.** Mix the cornflour and 3 tablespoons of cold water with a fork. Add the cornflour mix to the pan and allow the sauce to thicken.

**6.** Remove the pan from the heat and **taste adjust** to your palate.

**7.** In a salad bowl whisk together the English mustard, sesame oil and rice vinegar. Add the watercress and radish and toss the veg with the dressing.

**8.** Serve the mushrooms, shallots and peppers with the salad.

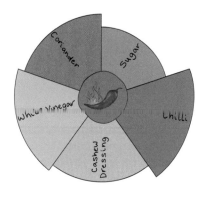

# Aubergine Vindaloo (Ve)

Vindaloo is one of the spicier curries you'll find on the menu of the local curry house; it's also very sour and has a boatload of garlic. This curry is all about hot and sour flavours. Originally from Goa, the vindaloo has a Portuguese influence. The voyagers marinated the meat in red wine, which eventually became vinegar during the journey. Today the red wine is swapped out for white vinegar. The traditional dish uses pork; however, I'm using aubergine because I think the texture of a fried aubergine is silky and beautiful. If some of your family aren't into spicy food cool everything down with Cashew and Tamarind Chutney (p. 251) or yoghurt.

SERVES 4

**Essential Equipment**
Large frying pan or wok

700g/1lb 8oz baby aubergines or 4 aubergines, cut into wedges
½ tsp ground turmeric
1 tsp salt
1 tbsp neutral oil

FOR THE SAUCE
90ml/3fl oz vegetable oil
¼ tsp black mustard seeds
½ tsp cumin seeds
1 red onion, sliced
2 tsp chilli powder (preferably Kashmiri)
2.5cm/1in piece of fresh ginger, minced
8 garlic cloves, minced
7 green finger chillies, sliced
1 tbsp tomato paste
½ tsp smoked paprika or paprika
1 tsp cayenne pepper
120ml/4fl oz white malt vinegar or cider vinegar
2 tsp sugar
Handful of chopped coriander

TO SERVE
Cashew and Tamarind Chutney (p. 251)

**1.** If you're using baby aubergines, slice halfway down each aubergine and then into quarters, keeping the top attached. If you're using a standard aubergine, simply cut into wedges. Mix together the turmeric, salt and oil, rub over the aubergines and allow to sit for 30 minutes. Wear gloves to do this otherwise your fingers might get a little stained.

**2.** Heat the oil over a medium heat in a wok or a large frying pan, and fry the aubergine with a slotted spoon. Work in batches and don't overcrowd your pan; semi-cook the aubergine and then set it aside to cool on kitchen paper, about 5–7 minutes per batch. You might need to add a little more oil between batches.

**3.** Using the same oil, increase the temperature. Check if the oil is hot enough by adding a couple of mustard seeds to the oil. The seeds should fizz lightly; if they don't, you need to wait longer for the oil to heat. Add the mustard and cumin seeds. Use a slotted spoon to agitate the spices and cover with a lid for 15–30 seconds until fragrant but not burnt.

**4.** Immediately add the red onion and Kashmiri chilli powder, and use the lid to shield yourself from the steam. Turn down the flame's heat, cover the pan and let the onions slowly caramelise for 10–12 minutes until they become deep golden brown.

**5.** Add in the ginger, garlic, green chillies, tomato paste, paprika and cayenne pepper and cook down for 2 minutes.

**6.** Ladle in 240ml/8fl oz of water, with the vinegar, sugar and fried aubergine. Cook the aubergine for 20 minutes or until softened, and then **taste adjust** to your palate. Serve with chopped coriander.

# Sichuan Fragrant Aubergine Tenders (Ve)

Sichuan fragrant aubergine or fish fragrant aubergine is a specialty in Sichuan. You might think this is a fish dish, but there is no fish involved in this recipe. The title is to do with its taste and the style of cooking. This flavour is based around the pickled chillies found in Sichuan chilli broad bean paste (doubanjiang) and is married with loads of garlic, ginger and spring onions. This sauce is sour, sweet and salty, and, of course, is Sichuanese so has to have a kick. This is my go-to if I'm looking for something punchy as it's quick to whip up.

**SERVES 2**

## Essential Equipment
Slotted spoon; wok or large pot

2 large aubergines, cut into
    2 x 10cm/4in batons
1 tbsp salt
200–300ml/7–11fl oz neutral oil
    for shallow frying
1 tsp Sichuan peppercorns,
    ground (optional)
1 tbsp Sichuan chilli broad bean
    paste (doubanjiang) or if you
    can't find it use 1½ tbsp
    gochujang
3 garlic cloves, minced
5cm/2in piece of ginger, minced
120ml/4fl oz vegetable stock
    or water
2 tsp sugar
1 tbsp soy sauce or tamari
1 tsp cornflour
2 tbsp Chinese black (Chinkiang)
    vinegar or rice wine vinegar
3 spring onions, sliced
Sprinkle of sesame seeds

**1.** In a large bowl mix the aubergine with the salt and leave for 30 minutes.

**2.** Wash the aubergine and pat dry with kitchen paper, then heat the oil in a wok to 180°C.

**3.** Add the aubergine to the oil and fry until golden and tender, about 5–10 minutes. Work in batches and don't overcrowd your pan. Remove the aubergine tenders with a slotted spoon and drain on kitchen paper.

**4.** Carefully remove the majority of the oil from the wok, leaving about 2 tablespoons in the pan. (Don't throw the oil down the sink, guys; put it in a small heatproof container and, once full, dispose of the oil safely.)

**5.** Over a medium heat add the Sichuan peppercorns and chilli broad bean paste, moving them around the pan until the oil is a deep red colour. Turn down the heat and add in the garlic and ginger. Fry for 1–2 minutes, making sure not to brown.

**6.** Add in the stock, sugar and soy sauce and bring to the boil.

**7.** Gently slide in your tender pieces of aubergine and simmer for 5 minutes until the sauce has come together.

**8.** Mix the cornflour with 2 tablespoons of cold water in a small bowl with a fork then add this to the pan. Gently stir the pan, making sure not to break up the aubergine, and allow the sauce to thicken. Finish with the Chinese black vinegar.

**9. Taste adjust** to your flavour profile.

**10.** Plate up and finish with sliced spring onions and sesame seeds.

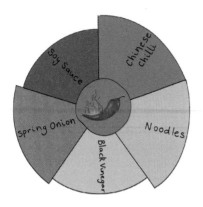

# Smoking Hot Noods

Over lockdown, while most were playing with banana bread and sourdough, I got really into noodles. I geeked out on the science of noodles because I really wanted to make hand-pulled noodles (La Mian); it turns out they're really hard. However, during this process, I did learn a lot about the gluten structure in noodles. It is the alkalinity of the noodle that strengthens the gluten, giving you that classic noodle chew. In China, kansui, an alkaline solution, is used; here, however, I'm using bicarbonate of soda, which does a good job and strengthens the gluten to make delicious, chewy noodles. If you don't have the time to make homemade noodles or don't have a pasta machine, skip to step 9 and buy some dried noodles, and you've got smoking hot oil noods in 10 minutes.

SERVES 2

**Essential Equipment**
Pasta machine (if making your own noods)

FOR THE NOODLES
300g/10½oz dried wheat
    noodles
OR
200g/7oz strong white bread
    flour (above 13% protein –
    see back of pack), plus extra
    for dusting
½ tsp salt
½ tsp bicarbonate of soda

2 pak choi, halved
2 tsp soy sauce
2 tsp Chinese black vinegar
    (Chinkiang)
1 garlic clove, minced
2–4 tsp crushed Chinese chilli
    flakes per bowl
Pinch of salt
4 spring onions, sliced
6 tbsp neutral oil

MAKING NOODLES

**1.** If you are making your own noodles dissolve the salt and bicarbonate of soda in 80ml/3fl oz water.

**2.** If using a stand mixer with a dough hook, add the flour to the bowl and add the water gradually in thirds, allowing the machine to process until the dough looks like small pebbles. If kneading by hand, use chopsticks and gradually add the water to the flour in a large bowl. Keep mixing until all the water is added; you should get a shaggy dough that is difficult to knead. If there any dry bits of flour, discard and don't add any more water.

**3.** Cover the dough and allow to rest for 30 mins.

**4.** Form the dough into a ball, divide it in half and keep one half covered. The dough will be quite stiff; try to roll it out as best you can using a rolling pin.

**5.** Put the dough through your pasta machine on the widest setting, passing the dough through entirely. Decrease the thickness and pass the dough through again; keep repeating until you have decreased four times in total. Take the dough and fold it in thirds, and repeat from 0–3 again, making sure the dough rolls through in the same direction. Do this one further time. Dust the sheet with flour then cover with cling film or a dry tea towel and leave to rest at room temperature for 30 minutes. Repeat with the second piece of dough.

**6.** Take the rested dough sheet and pass through the pasta machine, reducing the thickness sequentially until you get your desired thickness: approx. 2mm; on my machine it's setting 6.

**8.** Dust your sheet liberally in flour or cornflour to stop it sticking and roll the dough through the noodle cutter, catching the dough underneath the cutter as the noodles fall. Dust off the noodles. You can keep these noodles in the fridge uncovered for up to 3 days or store them frozen in sealed containers.

**9.** To make the hot oil noodles, bring a large saucepan of salted water to the boil.

**10.** Blanch the noodles with the pak choi for 2-4 minutes, or if using dried noodles, follow the cooking instructions and halfway through cooking the noodles, add the pak choi. Drain the noodles through a sieve and rinse under cold water for a few seconds, then divide between the serving bowls.

**11.** To each serving bowl, add 1 tsp soy sauce, ½ tsp Chinese black vinegar, ½ minced garlic clove, ½–1 tsp crushed Chinese chilli flakes (depending on your spice tolerance), a pinch of salt and the sliced spring onions.

**12.** Heat the oil in a saucepan until glossy, at about 120°C. Then *very carefully* pour the oil over the noodles, aiming for the garlic and chilli. Distribute the oil over both serving bowls – it will bubble up and foam.

**13.** Mix everything up really well, then enjoy your noods.

**14. Taste and adjust** to your palate.

**Note**
Once the noodles are cooked, wash them in clean water to stop them sticking.

**SCIENCE THINGS**

The gluten matrix is the structure of all doughs. This matrix has three main qualities:

**1.** Elastic – giving a springy texture
**2.** Extensible – allowing the dough to stretch
**3.** Viscous – shown when the dough relaxes

For noodle dough, we're looking for a highly elastic dough. Gluten is the protein content of the flour; the higher the gluten, the higher the protein. Therefore we need a high-gluten dough.

Bicarbonate of soda is alkaline; in an ideal case, we would be using baked bicarbonate of soda or lye. Raising the dough's pH increases the dough's firmness, giving the noodles a yellow colour and springy texture.

In China, lye (or kansui) is used, which has a higher pH. However, it's hard to source outside of Asia. As a substitute, you can bake bicarbonate of soda to form sodium carbonate: heat 50g/1½oz of bicarbonate of soda at 180°C for 2–5 hours until it has reduced to two thirds of its original weight. Do not touch bare skin with baked bicarbonate of soda as this is an irritant, and keep in an airtight container.

By running the dough through the pasta machine in the same direction, you align the gluten structure, creating a firmer, more extensible dough.

If you want to find out more on the science of noodles, Serious Eats has loads of great information.

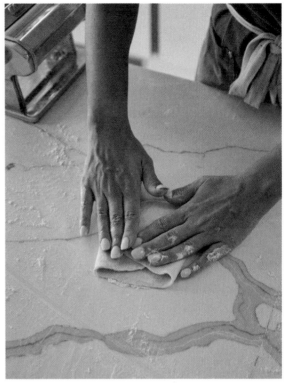

# Korean Chilli No-Knead Focaccia

I made sourdough bread for years; however, it does take sooo much time, you have to remember to feed your starter and the worst part is you do everything to the T and still you sometimes get a pancake – so disheartening. When it does go right it's amazing for the first day, then it's stale. Focaccia is completely the opposite: so satisfying, hard to mess up, and it lasts for ages because the olive oil preserves it. I'm adding gochujang because it tastes delish and it looks super cool. Have it on its own or as a sandwich.

MAKES 1 LOAF

**Essential Equipment**
23 x 33cm/9 x 13in oven tray or large cast-iron pan

512g/1lb 2oz strong white
   bread flour
1½ tsp salt
7g/¼oz instant yeast
455ml/15fl oz lukewarm water
4 tbsp extra virgin olive oil
2 tbsp gochujang
Sprinkle of flaky sea salt

HOW TO FOLD FOCACCIA

**1.** Mix the bread flour, salt and yeast and whisk together.

**2.** Slowly add in the lukewarm water and mix into a shaggy dough.

**3.** Place in a container at least double the size of the dough, add a tablespoon of olive oil on top to make sure the dough doesn't dry up and cover with cling film, a lid or a damp tea towel. Leave it to rise in the fridge overnight.

**4.** You can also let it rise at room temperature for 3–4 hours, but the flavour won't develop as well and it won't be as fluffy.

**5.** Line an oven tray or cast-iron pan with 1 tablespoon of olive oil.

**6.** Make the gochu glaze by mixing the gochujang with 1 tablespoon of olive oil.

**7.** Remove the dough from the fridge and punch it with your fist to push out the air.

**8.** Take the dough out of the container, place it on a clean surface and gently spread it out. Pour the glaze in the middle of the dough, then take each edge and pinch it into the middle, so you encase the glaze in the middle of the dough and seal the edge. Flip the whole thing over, place it in the oven tray and cover the tin with a damp cloth or cling film. Leave it to prove for 2–4 hours or until it has doubled in size and looks puffy.

**9.** Preheat the oven to 240°C (220°C fan oven) Gas 9.

**10.** Lightly drizzle 1 tablespoon of olive oil on the dough, then oil up your hands and lightly push your fingers into the dough to make deep dimples.

**11.** Add a sprinkle of flaky sea salt.

**12.** Bake for 25–30 minutes until the crust is golden. Remove from the oven and let it cool on a wire rack.

**13.** Slice and enjoy as it is or make the ultimate kimchi toastie.

**Tip**
This is one recipe that is hard to adjust as the dough ratio is pretty set. You can play with other glazes and herb additions.

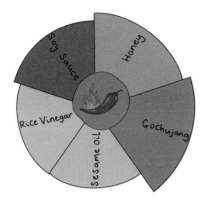

# Gochujang Spatchcock Chicken and Duck Fat Spicy Roasties

This gochujang spatchcock chicken is going to replace your classic roast dinner. The gochujang glaze beautifully coats the chicken and it's perfect for barbecue season. If you are wanting to whack this on your barbecue, cook at around 180–200°C over indirect heat until you get an internal temperature of 65°C, glazing every 10–12 minutes.

SERVES 4

**Essential Equipment**
Hot oven or barbecue;
pastry brush

FOR THE GOCHU-SPATCHCOCK
4 tbsp honey
4 tbsp soy sauce
2 tbsp rice vinegar
2 tbsp gochujang
2 tbsp sesame oil
1 free-range chicken, about
   1.5kg/3lb 5oz

FOR THE SPICY ROASTIES
1–1.5kg/2lb 3oz–2lb 9oz Maris
   Piper potatoes, peeled and
   quartered
200ml/7fl oz duck fat or
   neutral oil
Sprinkle of flaky sea salt
2 tsp togarashi or 1 tsp chilli
   powder and 1 tsp sesame
   seeds

HOW TO SPATCHCOCK A CHICKEN

**1.** In a small bowl mix the honey, soy, rice vinegar, gochujang and sesame oil and **taste adjust** to your palate. Be mindful, though, that too much honey will caramelise in the oven and blacken the chicken.

**2.** Place the chicken with the breasts facing down on a clean chopping board. Using kitchen scissors, cut down each side of the backbone and remove.

**3.** Flip the bird back over and press on the breast with the palm of your hand, letting the bird lie flat and tucking the wings under the rib cage to prevent burning. Place the chicken on a parchment-lined oven tray and brush a third of the marinade onto the chicken. Cover, refrigerate and allow to marinate for at least 1 hour or overnight.

**4.** Take the chicken out of the fridge and preheat the oven to 220°C (200°C fan oven) Gas 7.

**5.** Parboil the potatoes in salted water for 8–10 minutes and then remove and drain in a colander. Place the potatoes on a clean kitchen cloth over a cold oven tray to allow them to fully dry for 10 minutes – this is one of the secrets to crispy roasties. Place the potatoes back in the colander to rough up the edges.

**6.** Put a deep oven tray with the duck fat in the oven to heat up for 10 minutes.

**7.** Carefully remove the hot tray from the oven and place it on your hob. Add the cold potatoes to the fat using tongs – you should see them start to sizzle. Coat each potato in the fat before returning the tray to the oven. Turn down the heat to 200°C (180°C fan oven) Gas 6 and cook for 1 hour, turning every 20 minutes.

**8.** Remove the chicken from the fridge, place in the oven and roast for 40–50 minutes or until the temperature on your thermometer reads at least 65°C in the thickest part. Make sure to brush on the remaining marinade a third at a time every 10–12 minutes.

**9.** Check that the chicken and the potatoes are beautifully caramelised, otherwise turn up the oven to 220°C (200°C fan oven) Gas 7 until fully golden.

**10.** Take the chicken and the potatoes out of the oven. Remove the potatoes from the tray and place in a large bowl, and season with flaky sea salt and togarashi.

**11.** Allow the chicken to rest for 10 minutes before carving.

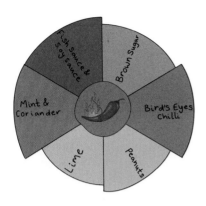

# Vietnamese-Inspired Caramelised Pork Bowls

**You know that overused spag bol or chilli con carne that you love but are a little tired of? Let me introduce the caramelised pork bowl. It's ready in under 30 minutes and it's super, SUPER tasty.**

SERVES 4

**Essential Equipment**
Wok or large frying pan

2 tbsp neutral oil
6 spring onions, sliced, white
  and green parts separately
2 carrots, grated or finely
  chopped (I like to use a
  mandoline but be careful)
Pinch of salt
2.5cm/1in piece of ginger, minced
4 garlic cloves, minced
4–8 bird's eye or Thai chillies,
  finely sliced
500g/1lb 1½oz pork, minced
5 tbsp/60g/2oz brown sugar
3 tbsp fish sauce
3 tbsp soy sauce
1 tsp chilli flakes
3 tbsp roasted peanuts, crushed
1 lime, wedged
Handful of coriander, chopped
Handful of mint, chopped

TO SERVE
Steamed jasmine rice

**1.** If you're serving with rice, get your rice on the go first.

**2.** Heat a wok over a medium-high heat with the oil, then add the spring onions (white parts only), half the carrots and the salt. Cook for 3–4 minutes, stirring constantly. You're looking for the carrot to turn slightly limp. Add the ginger, garlic and chillies and cook for a further minute until aromatic.

**3.** Add the pork mince to the wok and turn up to a high heat, breaking up all the meat with a spatula to make sure all the pork turns white and there are no pink bits.

**4.** Add the brown sugar, fish sauce and soy sauce. Give everything a stir before leaving it to fully cook down and caramelise without stirring for about 6–8 minutes. Stir again and then let everything fully caramelise again for about 60 seconds. Repeat until the meat is dark brown and there are little crispy bits of pork. However, keep an eye on it because it can burn quickly.

**5. Taste adjust** to your flavour profile, and serve over rice with chilli flakes, the rest of the spring onions, roasted peanuts, lime wedges and chopped fresh herbs.

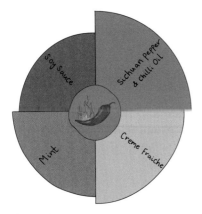

# *Fancy* Sichuan Lamb Chops with Chilli Oil Crispy Potatoes

Visiting Xi'an Muslim quarter is my favourite food memory. There are hundreds of different street foods in the area but my favourite had to be the cumin and chilli crusted lamb skewers. The lamb is skewered and cooked over charcoal. The meat is liberally dusted in layers of cumin and chilli powder that create a beautiful spiced crust. The lamb fat instantly popped in my mouth, coating my tongue with cumin, chilli heat. I made my way through the rest of the skewers in a matter of minutes – my tummy was so content. These lamb chops are inspired by the classic Xinjiang lamb kebabs.

SERVES 4

**Essential Equipment**
Pestle and mortar, spice grinder or end of a rolling pin (to blend spices with)

FOR THE LAMB
1½ tbsp soy sauce
1½ tbsp Shaoxing wine or sherry wine
1 tsp salt
8–12 lamb cutlets or chops
1½ tbsp cumin seeds
½ tsp Sichuan chilli flakes or gochugaru (Korean chilli flakes)
1 tsp Sichuan peppercorns
3 tbsp neutral oil

FOR THE CHILLI OIL BABY POTS
600g/1lb 5oz baby potatoes
100ml/3½fl oz neutral oil
3 tbsp Philli's Chilli Oil (p. 250) or 2 tbsp shop-bought chilli oil
1 tsp flaky salt (preferably Maldon)
3 tbsp crème fraîche
Small handful of mint, chopped

**1.** Mix the soy sauce, Shaoxing wine and salt in a bowl and add the lamb. Leave to marinate for at least 2 hours but preferably overnight, covered, in the fridge.

**2.** Preheat the oven to 220°C (200°C fan oven) Gas 7.

**3.** Bring a large pan of salted water to the boil. Cook the potatoes uncovered for 20–25 minutes until they are fully cooked, then drain through a colander and make sure they're dried off for about 5 minutes.

**4.** Place the potatoes on an oven tray and use a masher or a large fork to gently crush each one. The thinner the crispier they will be; the thicker the fluffier. Make sure the tray is not over-crowded. Drizzle each potato with neutral oil and chilli oil and then sprinkle with flaky salt.

**5.** Cook the potatoes in the oven for 25–30 minutes until fully crisp.

**6.** Meanwhile, remove the lamb from the fridge. Take the cumin seeds, chilli flakes and Sichuan peppercorns and crush them with a pestle and mortar or a spice grinder. Coat the lamb in the three-quarters of the spice mix.

**7.** Heat a good glug of neutral oil in a frying pan over a medium-high heat and make sure the pan looks glossy. Add the lamb cutlets and cook for 2 minutes on each side before removing. The internal temperature should be just over 50°C. Allow the lamb to rest.

**8.** Remove the potatoes from the oven.

**9.** Serve the lamb and potatoes with a drizzle of crème fraîche and some freshly chopped mint, and finish the lamb with a dusting of the spice blend.

**10. Taste** and make any adjustments. If you want more spice, load on the chilli oil; or if it's too much, cool it down with more crème fraîche.

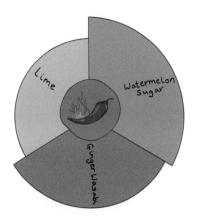

SERVES 8

**Essential Equipment**
Blender or stick blender

1 small watermelon, approx.
   1kg/2lb 3oz, peeled and
   deseeded
Juice of 2 limes
5cm/2in piece of ginger,
   peeled and chopped
½ tbsp wasabi
65g/2oz sugar
Zest of 1 lime
½ shot gin or tequila per bowl
   (optional)

NOTE
If you want to hold the booze
just leave it out.

# Watermelon and Wasabi Snow Cone with Lime Ⓥᵉ

**Whip this snow cone out at the end of a dinner party and you might be singing Carly Rae Jepsen till 4am.**

**1.** Remove the rind of the watermelon. Blend the watermelon with the lime juice, ginger, wasabi and sugar and strain through a sieve into a freezerproof container.

**2. Taste and adjust** to your palate with more ginger, wasabi, sugar or lime, however don't alter too much as it'll affect the texture of the granita.

**3.** Freeze for 2–3 hours and scrape the surface layer. After another 2 hours scrape again and continue until all the ice is scraped and you have completely frozen granita.

**4.** Alternatively, you can completely freeze the block, lightly defrost the outside of the container under a hot tap and chop the block into cubes using a hot serrated knife and quickly blend, but only do this if your blender can handle ice.

**5.** Store in the freezer until ready to use.

**6.** Store your serving bowls in the freezer to stop the granita melting.

**7.** Serve in frozen bowls with lime zest and pour over half a shot of alcohol per bowl.

# COMFORT

Comforting foods are the rich indulgent foods that make you feel safe and cosy inside. Comfort is a bit of me, it's bao, dumplings and decadent black bean mahkani. This one is a must! Embrace your love of carbs.

We all hear chefs saying on the telly that fat equals flavour, and while that is true it's a little more complex than we might think. Fats are great for dissolving and concentrating flavours that are released into the air when heated, which is why you can smell bacon filling the air on a Sunday morning. Fats dissolve into other fats –that's why as your bacon slowly renders it gets beautiful and crisp. **Side note: as animal fats render at 180°C you're probably safer sticking the bacon on an oven tray and roasting it, as misuse of a frying pan can send it from flabby to black in minutes.**

Fats are also great for dissolving seasonings and salt; for example, olive oil makes for great salad dressings. Fats like extra virgin olive oil have some volatile flavour compounds that are lost to the air during cooking, so shouldn't be cooked with. Acid balances fat, like the way vinegar and olive oil work in harmony in a dressing.

Sugars and proteins in animal fats, like butter and the outer crust on a sirloin steak, oxidise and caramelise to form more complex flavours like nutty brown butter (see the BBBR on page 130 for an example of this). Fat is not only a flavour, it's a cooking medium. We use fats to cook with because they can be heated to high temperatures way above boiling points, and this is key to rendering fat and getting those crispy bits. When cooking a piece of meat or mushrooms in a frying pan you should always wait for the pan to be super hot. I prefer using heavy frying pans like cast iron because they retain their heat and are ovenproof. You can test if the pan is hot by adding a few drops of water; they should dance around the pan before evaporating. When you add the oil to the pan, it should look shiny and glossy. Then when you add the meat or shrooms to the pan it should create a loud sizzle. If this doesn't happen, remove the meat with some tongs and wait a little longer.

I love the fat on the end of a sirloin or a rack of lamb, but that was not always the case. Too many times I discarded the white flabby edge of a piece of meat because it was chewy and unpleasant. This is because this fat was not rendered. Rendering fat completely changes it and it transforms into melty, flavourful bites. The fat on a steak also needs to be seasoned more heavily because salt doesn't dissolve as easily in the fat. Once the meat is fully cooked, but before it's rested, hold the meat with tongs or engineer a contraption with a wooden spoon and a spatula to sit the meat on its edge to gently crisp up that delicious fat.

Meat contains more fat than veggies: I learned all about this when first cooking vegan food. Derek Sarno, a leader of plant-based cooking, uses more oils in his cooking than you might think. This is because a piece of steak has layers of fat running through the meat and gently bastes itself while cooking, however a mushroom is 80 per cent water, so although it takes on salt a lot more easily, it does need a little help from vegetable oils to absorb the fat during cooking.

Some studies say that fat is not one of the core tastes, nor can you smell it. However, there are some opposing studies that argue fat does have a taste that is similar to a bitter flavour if tasted alone, and that fat is the sixth taste. The problem is that fat often works in harmony with creaminess and it's difficult for our minds to distinguish between fat and creaminess, as they are frequently perceived as one flavour. We experience creaminess via a combination of chemical detection, smell and taste, and physical mechanisms via the nerve endings on your tongue feeling the micro globules of fat in suspension in a liquid. Plus we use sight to see what we have previously experienced to be creamy.

Fat carries more energy per gram than any other food group, which is why fat makes us feel fuller. Being full triggers the release of a hormone that makes us feel relaxed and content. This could be an evolutionary adaptation as the caveman or cavewoman inside us has their full tummy after grafting for days to find that meal. You can now blame them for that craving for Katsu chicken (please see p. 144 to satisfy your inner caveman or cavewoman).

You can find Comfort food found throughout Asia. I love chomping through nasi goreng in Bali, slurping dumplings in Shaolin and munching squishy bao in Taipei. Although all of these dishes are very different they all make me feel warm, soothed and comforted.

## Comfort ingredients

- Paneer
- Coconut milk
- Oils
- Sesame
- Bao
- Cheese
- Peanut butter
- Tahini
- Butter/ghee
- Dumplings
- Coconut oil
- Nuts
- Cream
- Noodles and pasta

# My Mum's Chapatis (Ve)

Okay, so you might think that my passion for food came from my mum, as she was brought up in Mumbai. This was not the case; my mum is a lot of great things, but cooking did not come into it. There was always a shortcut in the household – this is probably where my impatience for cooking came from. Instead of learning how to master spices from a young age, we would get our family orders from the local curry house. However, like many Indian mothers, my mum is smart with her money. That meant we made the chapatis, rice and lentils at home. The chapati dough was kneaded and rolled before being cooked on a hot pan, just in time for our delicious curries to arrive with the doorbell.

SERVES 4/MAKES 12 CHAPATIS

**Essential Equipment**
Large heavy-based frying pan;
stepped spatula

270g/9½oz plain flour,
    plus extra for rolling
1 tsp salt
2 tsp neutral oil

ROLLING CHAPATIS

**1.** Put the flour, salt and oil into a bowl and mix with your hand.

**2.** Start adding 150ml/5½fl oz water bit by bit. You want the dough to fully come together and feel soft. You might need a little more or less water depending on your flour.

**3.** Knead the dough for 10 minutes before covering with a damp cloth and leaving for 20 minutes.

**4.** Divide the dough into 12 equal pieces (about 35g/1oz each) and cover again with the damp cloth.

**5.** Roll each piece of dough into a ball and then flatten with your palm. Dust the flattened dough on both sides with flour and then, using a rolling pin, roll out to a diameter of 12–15cm/5–6in. Keep dusting in flour if the dough starts to stick.

**6.** Place a large heavy frying pan over a high heat and dust off any excess flour.

**7.** Add the chapati and cook for 30 seconds, then flip the bread and cook until you see brown spots on the underside. Flip a final time and press down over the top of the chapati with a stepped spatula: the bread should puff and fill with steam.

**8.** Take the chapati off the heat and place it in a dry tea towel to keep warm while you cook the remaining chapatis.

**9.** If eating later, reheat the chapatis, brush with a little water and wrap in foil before popping in a preheated oven at 180°C for 5 minutes.

**Tip**
My mum got me to help her make the chapatis because it's a lot easier to roll and then cook each bread. If you're cooking solo, roll the chapatis, making sure to place a piece of baking parchment between each layer to stop them sticking, and cover the top one with a damp tea towel.

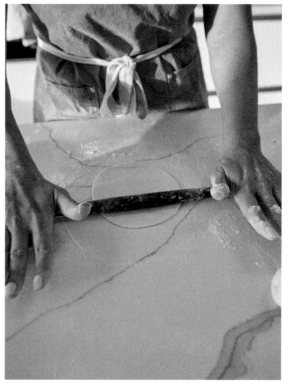

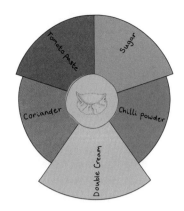

# Black Bean Makhani

Dahl makhani from New Delhi is what is mac and cheese is to America, and it's my go-to order at Dishoom. Makhani means buttery, and you'll often find this dish front and centre at special occasions as it's pure indulgence. This dahl is traditionally made from urad dal, which is not a lentil but actually tiny, black mung beans. Urad dal is hard to source so I've amended this recipe with black turtle beans; it's quicker and I think just as tasty.

SERVES 4

**Essential Equipment**
Saucepan

50g/1½oz unsalted butter
1 cinnamon stick (optional)
1 red onion, finely diced
6 garlic cloves, minced
5cm/2in piece of ginger, minced
60g/2oz tomato paste
1 tsp fine sea salt
1 tsp Kashmiri chilli powder or
⅔ tsp chilli powder
450g/1lb tinned black beans,
drained (2 tins)
100ml/3½fl oz double cream,
plus extra for drizzling
(optional)
1 tsp garam masala
1 tsp sugar
Coriander, to garnish

**1.** Melt the butter in a large saucepan over a medium heat. When foamy add in the cinnamon stick and cook for 2 minutes until you can smell the cinnamon.

**2.** Add the onion, garlic, ginger, tomato paste, salt and chilli powder. Fry off for 5 minutes until the onions are translucent.

**3.** Drain the beans and add to the pan with 500ml/18fl oz of water to cover the beans. Bring to the boil and then cook over a medium heat for 25 minutes or until all the liquid is nearly gone, stirring occasionally.

**4.** Add in the cream, garam masala and sugar, cook for a further 15 minutes and then **taste adjust** to your palate.

**5.** If you want to finish it off with a little more decadence, top it with an extra drizzle of cream and chopped coriander.

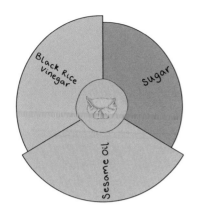

**Essential Equipment**
Rolling pin; steamer or frying pan
with lid

FOR THE DUMPLING WRAPPERS
36 shop-bought dumpling
    wrappers
OR
320g/11½oz plain flour
¼ teaspoon salt
2 tbsp neutral oil, for frying

FOR THE FILLING
2 tbsp sesame oil
½ head of cabbage, shredded
    (about 250g/9oz)
125g/4½oz shitake or chestnut
    mushrooms, diced
125g/5oz firm tofu, drained and
    diced
2.5cm/1in piece of ginger, minced
¼ tsp salt
½ tsp ground white pepper
1 tbsp soy sauce or tamari
1 tbsp cornflour mixed with
    3 tbsp water

FOR THE SAUCE
4 tbsp sesame oil
2 tbsp black rice vinegar or
    white rice vinegar
1 tsp sugar
1 tbsp hot water
1 tsp sesame seeds

# Women of Shaolin Cabbage Dumplings with Sesame Dressing (Ve)

You might have heard of Shaolin before thanks to its Buddhist monks or kung fu. It was on my bucket list when I when to China. I made my way to Shaolin from Gubeikou, camping in a watch tower on the Great Wall of China (I think this might be illegal so I don't advise doing this, however it is pretty amazing). Having woken up at sunrise, I made my way via various bus journeys back to Beijing, where I had to buy a ticket to Shaolin. Unfortunately, I'd chosen a public holiday to travel so all the seated train tickets had sold out. Yup, I put on my big girl pants and, using my camping mat from the night before as a pillow, I settled in for a long night in the aisle on the sleeper train. I am quite proud of my sleeping abilities, however the nice tea lady insisted on running the trolley down the aisle every 30 minutes, meaning sleep was limited. Arriving in Shaolin in the early hours of the morning made it all worth it. From the window, I saw literally thousands of children training in kung fu, all moving in harmony. I made my way through this magical town via the temple and found the homestay. When I entered, I was greeted by three generations of women from the family who were busy making dumplings. I asked if I could help, in a pointy fashion as I know literally nothing in Mandarin. These women showed me how they made their family dumplings in Shaolin and I would like to share their recipe with you.

**1.** To make the dumpling wrappers mix the plain flour, salt and neutral oil with 175ml/6fl oz just-boiled water.

**2.** If kneading by hand, bring the dough together to distribute the moisture with a wooden spoon or chopsticks, then knead on a surface for 2–3 minutes, place in a clean bowl, cover and leave for 30–45 minutes. If using a stand mixer knead for 2 minutes before resting, covered.

**3.** Make the filling by heating a frying pan over a medium heat with the sesame oil and adding the cabbage and mushrooms. Fry until cooked down for about 5 minutes.

**4.** Add in the tofu, ginger, salt, pepper and soy sauce and cook for 2 minutes. Crush up the tofu in the pan with a potato masher or large fork and evaporate most of the liquid. Whisk 1 tablespoon of cornflour with 3 tablespoons of cold water and add to the pan and allow the mixture to thicken.

**5.** Remove the filling and place in a bowl to cool slightly.

**6.** Take out the dough for the wrappers; you'll notice it's a lot more workable.

**7.** Poke a hole in the middle of the dough and work into a large doughnut ring. Cut the dough into 32 pieces about 12g/½oz each and re-cover with a damp cloth.

**8.** Roll a piece of dough into a ball with the heel of your hand and dust it with flour. Then use a rolling pin to roll out the dough into a smooth circle. Keeping the rolling pin on the surface, lightly press the wrapper's edges and rotate the dough using your other hand by about 30 degrees. The wrapper should be about 8cm/3½in in diameter at the end, and the edges are thinner than the middle of the wrapper. Dust the wrapper with flour and store under a clean, dry towel to prevent the wrapper from drying out. Repeat with the rest of the dough pieces. Do not stack them otherwise they'll stick to each other.

**9.** To fold the dumplings, place a teaspoon of filling in the centre of the wrapper. Fold the middle of the wrapper to make a half circle. Then make a triangle by pinching each remaining corner inwards to the middle. Pinch the middle with your three fingers.

**10.** To cook the dumplings, steam the dumplings for 12 minutes over a medium heat in a lined steamer basket or heat a large non-stick frying pan with the oil and place a layer of dumplings in the pan. Allow them to caramelise and become golden. Add 100ml/3½fl oz water, quickly put on the lid and let the dumplings steam until all the water has evaporated, about 5–7 minutes. Do not overcrowd the pan and work in batches.

**11.** Remove the lid and allow the water to evaporate, then gently take out the dumplings from the pan. Use a stepped spatula to gently remove any dumpling that sticks.

**12.** Whisk the all the ingredients for the dumpling sauce, **taste and adjust** to your palate.

**13.** Serve the dumplings with the dressing in small saucers or completely drench the dumplings in the sauce.

**Tip**
You can store the dumplings in the freezer raw if you want to keep a quick scooby snack prepped and ready.

ROLL AND FOLD DUMPLINGS

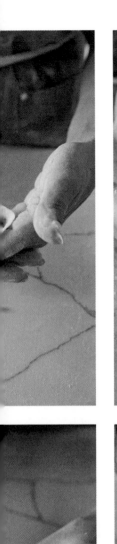

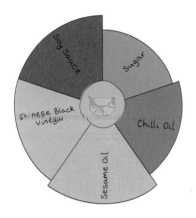

# Sausage Meat Wontons with the Perfect Dumpling Dressing

I LOVE dumplings; I would have them as a food group if I could. The beauty of this dumpling recipe is that you can make a batch and keep them in the freezer, then you have a quick, delicious meal that's super speedy. I'll be making the dumpling wrappers, but no judgement if you don't have the time to make them; just pop to your local Asian specialist shop and pick up a pack of dumpling wrappers. Then you can skip to the filling stage.

The sauce in this recipe is the real hero; in short, it has *all* the flavours. It's your chance to experiment and adjust to your taste.

SERVES 4/MAKES 36–40
DUMPLINGS

**Essential Equipment**
Rolling pin; frying pan with lid

FOR THE DUMPLING WRAPPERS
36 dumpling wrappers
OR
320g/11½oz plain flour
¼ teaspoon salt
2 tbsp neutral oil, for frying

FOR THE FILLING
6 large sausages, casings
　removed, or 400g/14oz
　sausage meat
4 spring onions, sliced
5cm/2in ginger, minced
1 tbsp soy sauce
½ tbsp sesame oil
¼ tsp white pepper (optional)
½ tsp Sichuan peppercorns,
　ground (optional)

FOR THE DRESSING
1 tsp sugar
3 tbsp soy sauce
3 tbsp Chinese black vinegar
　(Chinkiang) or rice vinegar
1 tsp Philli's Chilli Oil (p. 250)
　or shop-bought chilli oil
1 garlic clove, minced
1 tsp sesame seeds
2 tsp sesame oil

**1.** Make the dumpling wrappers as per steps 1–2 on p. 122.

**2.** Mix the sausage meat with the spring onion, ginger, soy sauce, sesame oil, white pepper (if using) and Sichuan peppercorns (if using).

**3.** Roll out the dumpling wrappers as per steps 6–8 on p. 124.

**4.** To fold the dumplings, place about a teaspoon (12g/½oz) of meat filling in the centre of the wrapper. Pinch the middle of the wrapper to make a half circle. Pleat 3 or 4 folds on each side, starting in the centre and moving outwards. For detailed step-by-step photos and video on how to roll and fold the dumplings please see (p.125–7). Press the edges into a half-moon circle. You can store the raw dumplings in the freezer if you want to keep a quick Scooby snack prepped and ready.

**5.** To cook the dumplings, heat a large non-stick frying pan with the oil and place a layer of dumplings in the pan. Allow to caramelise and become golden. Add 100ml/3½fl oz water, quickly pop on the lid and let the dumplings steam until all the water has evaporated, about 5–7 minutes.

**6.** Remove the lid, allow the water to evaporate then gently take out the dumplings from the pan. Use a stepped spatula if any dumpling sticks.

**7.** Whisk all the ingredients for the dressing with 1 tablespoon of hot water. **Taste and adjust** to your palate.

**8.** Serve with the dumpling dressing in small saucers or completely drench the dumplings in the sauce.

# BBBR: Brown Butter Basmati Rice

To be clear, most food is better with butter, specifically brown butter. I love rice and the only thing I can think of to make it better is brown butter. Nutty, rich, indulgent, this is the best rice dish ever.

SERVES 4

**Essential Equipment**
Large pan with lid

50g/1½oz unsalted butter
300g/10½oz washed rice
½ tsp ground turmeric
1 tsp salt
Juice of ½ lemon

TO SERVE
Crispy Things (p. 252) or shop-
   bought crispy onions

**1.** Heat a saucepan over a medium heat, add the butter and cook until the butter is melted and starts to turn golden brown and smell nutty. Immediately take off the heat – if you cook too long you'll have burnt butter. Allow the butter to cool slightly.

**2.** Wash the rice in cold water in a large bowl, scrunching the grains with your hands to remove the starch. Then drain in a sieve until the water runs clear.

**3.** Add the washed rice, turmeric, salt and 500ml/18fl oz water to the brown butter. Heat over a high heat until just boiling.

**4.** Then put the lid on, lower the heat and cook for 10–12 minutes or until all the water is absorbed.

**5.** Once all the water has been absorbed and the rice is fully cooked turn off the heat and leave the pan to fully cool down without removing the lid for 5–10 minutes. This is the secret to fluffy rice.

**6.** Squeeze over the lemon juice. **Taste and adjust;** if it's a little too comforting add a bit more lemon juice. Serve with Crispy Things (p. 252) scattered over the top.

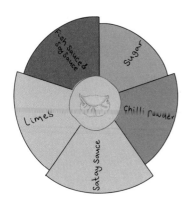

# Satay Prawns

Satay brings memories of beautiful beaches, scuba diving and Thai whisky buckets with those little bottles of supercharged Red Bull. If you know, you know. Prawns are great for a barbecue however if you don't have one you can blow torch the heads to add a little extra smokiness.

SERVES 4 AS A STARTER/
5–6 PRAWNS EACH

### Essential Equipment
Bamboo skewers (or just whack the prawns in a bowl)

500g/1lb 1½oz/24 raw tiger
   or king prawns
3 tbsp oil
1 tbsp fish sauce or ½ tbsp
   soy sauce
2 garlic cloves, minced
2 tsp ground turmeric
1 tsp ground coriander
1 tsp chilli powder
½ tsp salt, or more to taste
1 tbsp sugar or honey

TO SERVE
No-Cook Satay Sauce (p. 252)
1 lime, wedged

DE-POOPING PRAWNS

**1.** Soak the bamboo skewers in cold water for at least an hour.

**2.** Peel and devein the prawns. If you have prawns with their heads still on, don't remove the heads; they look great and are delicious to suck on.

**3.** Mix the oil, fish sauce, garlic, spices, salt and sugar together.

**4.** Rub over the prawns and allow to sit for 20 minutes.

**5.** Make the No-cook Satay Sauce (p. 252)

**6.** Take each prawn from the marinade and thread onto the skewers.

**7.** Heat a large frying pan and cook the skewers on each side for 2–3 minutes until the prawns start to turn orange.

**8.** Serve the prawns with the satay sauce and fresh lime wedges.

**Taste and adjust**
Add a squeeze of lime if it's too rich or a splash of fish sauce if you want more umami.

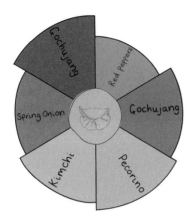

# Red Pepper and Kimchi Rigatoni

It's time to shake up your tired pasta night. Carbonara, spag bol, lasagne, caponata – leave them alone. This spicy red pepper dish is my go-to when I'm making pasta. No, it's not in any way traditional, but does that really matter when it's banging, and takes less than 15 minutes to make?

SERVES 4

**Essential Equipment**
Large frying pan; slotted spoon

350g/12½oz rigatoni, dried, or another type of pasta
2 tbsp extra virgin olive oil
120g/4oz chorizo, diced or 2 tbsp chilli oil to make it veggie
200g/7oz How I Kimchi (p. 162) or shop-bought kimchi, chopped
340g/12oz antipasti red peppers, sliced
4 garlic cloves, minced
4 eggs
2 tbsp gochujang
50g/1½oz pecorino, finely grated, plus extra to serve
½ tsp black pepper
4 spring onions, finely sliced

**1.** Cook the pasta in salted boiling water until al dente, about 11 minutes.

**2.** Put the oil and chorizo in a large frying pan and cook over a medium heat for 5–7 minutes until the fat comes out of the chorizo. If you're using chilli oil instead, wait to the end and drizzle it over the pasta to serve. Add in the kimchi and red peppers and fry off for 2 minutes.

**3.** Whisk together the garlic, eggs, gochujang, pecorino and black pepper.

**4.** Once the pasta is cooked, remove from the boiling water and add to the frying pan with a little pasta water. Turn the frying pan heat down to low and add the whisked egg mixture.

**5.** Gently stir together until the sauce thickens.

**6. Taste and adjust** to your palate.

**7.** Take off the heat and serve with sliced spring onions and more pecorino.

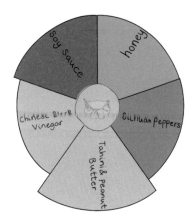

# Cuddly Dan Dan Noods

Dan dan noodles is a Sichuanese street food, meaning it's effing spicy. The traditional dan dan I found and ate in the streets of Chengdu are like fire, with enough numbing Sichuan peppercorns to make you think you have just been to the dentist. I have dialled down the spice and increased the creamy tahini and peanut butter to make this dish super comforting. Traditionally dan dan uses fermented mustard greens (sui mi ya cai), but they can be tricky to source. I love crispy capers and actually prefer them in this particular dish, however if you want to try the mustard greens too, simply swap for the capers.

SERVES 4

**Essential Equipment**
Wok or large frying pan

FOR THE SPICED MINCED BEEF
4 tbsp neutral oil
30g/1oz capers or sui mi ya cai
200g/7oz minced (ground) beef
  (> 15% fat) or pork mince
2 tsp hoisin sauce
1 tbsp Shaoxing wine or sherry
1 tsp soy sauce
¼ tsp five-spice powder

FOR THE SAUCE
3 tbsp tahini or sesame paste
3 tbsp smooth peanut butter
2 tbsp soy sauce
2 tbsp Chinese black vinegar
  (Chinkiang) or rice vinegar
2 tsp honey or sugar
2 garlic cloves, minced
½ tsp Sichuan peppercorns,
  ground (optional)
2 tbsp Philli's Chilli Oil (p. 250) or
  shop-bought chilli oil

FOR THE NOODLES AND VEG
400g/14oz fresh or 300g/10½oz
  dried noodles
Handful of choy sum, bok choi or
  tenderstem broccoli
1 tbsp roasted peanuts, crushed
3 spring onions, finely sliced

**1.** Heat 2 tablespoons of the oil in a wok or pan. Drain the capers from the brine and dry on kitchen paper. Add the capers to the hot oil and fry for 2–3 minutes until golden, then remove and set aside on a plate. Be careful as they can spit oil.

**2.** Heat another 2 tablespoons of oil in a wok or pan over a high heat and add the beef. Cook until there are no pink bits left.

**3.** Add in the hoisin, Shaoxing, soy sauce and five-spice and cook until all the liquid has evaporated. Then remove from the heat and reserve until you're ready to serve.

**4.** Mix all the sauce ingredients together with 60ml/2fl oz hot water, then **taste and adjust** to your palate. It should be super rich and nutty with a spicy kick.

**5.** Bring a large saucepan of salted water to the boil and cook the noodles and green vegetables for 2–3 minutes if using fresh. If using dried, cook the noodles as per packet instructions and add the green veggies 2–3 minutes before cooked. Strain the cooked noodles and veggies, reserving 200ml/7fl oz of noodle water, and wash the noodles with fresh water.

**6.** Divide the peanut sauce among the bowls, and add the noodles and the leafy greens. Pour over 50ml/1½fl oz per bowl of noodle water. Add the cooked beef and crispy capers and garnish with roast peanuts and spring onions.

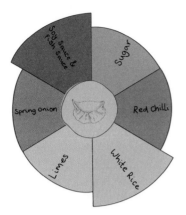

# Egg and Bacon Nasi Goreng
## (Indonesian-Inspired Fried Rice)

**Eggs and bacon aren't just for breakfast; you can have this indulgent rice for breakfast, lunch, dinner or at 3am. I love toasting the rice grains in rendered bacon. The trick to fried rice is using day-old rice, which means this dish is great for leftovers, so have a play if you have some mushies or broc in your veg draw to use up.**

SERVES 4

**Essential Equipment**
Wok or large frying pan

2 tbsp neutral oil
4 bacon rashers or 200g/7oz mushrooms, sliced into thin strips
1 red chilli, finely chopped
4 garlic cloves, minced
1 onion, diced
800g/1lb 12oz cooked day-old white rice
2 tbsp soy sauce
1 tbsp white sugar
2 tbsp fish sauce (optional)
2 spring onions, sliced
4 eggs

TO SERVE
Funky Chilli Sauce (p. 249) or sriracha
Sticky soy glaze (p. 248) or Kejap Manis
Crispy Things (p. 252) or crispy shallots
Lime wedges (optional)

**1.** Heat a wok or large frying pan over a medium-high heat. Add 1 tablespoon of neutral oil and the bacon and fry until crisp.

**2.** Add the chilli, garlic and onion and cook for 2 minutes.

**3.** Add the cooked rice and toast off the grains, keeping the rice moving with a spoon.

**4.** Add in the soy sauce, sugar and fish sauce.

**5.** Mix through half the spring onions and take off the heat.

**6. Taste and adjust** to your palate, then reserve until you're ready to serve.

**7.** Heat a separate non-stick frying pan, add a tablespoon of neutral oil then cook the eggs on high to get crispy edges.

**8.** Divide the rice between four bowls and top with the fried eggs, a drizzle of hot sauce and sticky soy glaze, crispy shallots and the rest of the spring onions. Serve with lime wedges.

# My Squishy Bao

I have a love affair with bao: I adore them but they can be a pain to make. I've tried countless recipes, read hundreds of research papers and made many failed attempts (one of which got me kicked off *MasterChef*.) I've finally cracked it with this recipe, and have tried to simplify everything into a foolproof method. It's based on southern-style Chinese steam buns and made with medium protein content, 9.5–11.0% (look on the back of the flour bag). If you don't want to have the faff or don't have a steamer, pick up some bao from the supermarket; however there's nothing quite like a fresh, steamy, squishy bao.

SERVES 4/MAKES 12 HIRATA BAO

**Essential Equipment**
Steamer or large wok with lid and trivet; baking parchment; pastry brush

2½ tsp instant dried yeast
1 tbsp neutral oil
600g/1lb 5oz plain flour
1½ tsp baking powder
40g/1½oz sugar
½ tsp salt

TO SERVE
The Secret Katsu Dunkers (p. 144) or Satay Prawns (p. 132), or if you're feeling super decadent, slices of Hong Kong-Style Pork Belly (p. 67) and Quick Pickled Cucs (p. 161)

MAKING BAO

**1.** Mix the yeast, oil and 300ml/11fl oz water at room temp and let it stand for 10 minutes.

**2.** Mix the dry ingredients (flour, baking powder, sugar and salt) in a large bowl.

**3.** Add the liquid yeast to the dry ingredients. If using a stand mixer, knead with a dough hook on low for 12–15 minutes. If kneading by hand, mix in the yeast and roughly knead into a dough. Leave the rough dough covered for 15 minutes. Come back and knead the dough for 10–20 minutes or until it feels smooth and elastic.

**4.** Leave the dough to prove in a clean bowl covered with a damp tea towel until it's doubled in size, about 1–2 hours.

**5.** Cut 12 x 5cm/2in squares of baking parchment.

**6.** Punch out the air from the dough, divide it into 12 equal portions and roll them into balls. Keep all the dough balls covered with a towel.

**7.** Roll out each dough ball into a long oval, brush with oil and fold over into a taco shape, then place on a baking parchment square and leave, covered, to prove for 15–30 minutes until the dough looks puffy. To test, press lightly into the dough: it should leave an indentation and slowly spring back. If it springs back quickly it needs more time; if it doesn't spring back, it's over proved.

**8.** If using a metal steamer, wrap the lid in a cloth to prevent burn spots. (If using a bamboo steamer, you don't need to worry about this.) If you don't have space in the steamer to cook all the buns at once, place the rest of the buns in the fridge to slow the proving.

9. Place the buns in the steamer, leaving space in between each bun and steam over a medium heat for 12 minutes.

10. Do not remove the lid, but turn off the heat, and wait for a further 5 minutes.

11. Remove the buns and serve immediately or let them cool on a wire rack.

12 To serve simply re-steam for 5 minutes or microwave for 1 minute.

**Tip**
You can store the buns in the freezer for up to 3 months. Steam from frozen for 5 minutes.

**Note**
I wouldn't advise altering this recipe as it's a bread recipe and this can affect the structure of the dough.

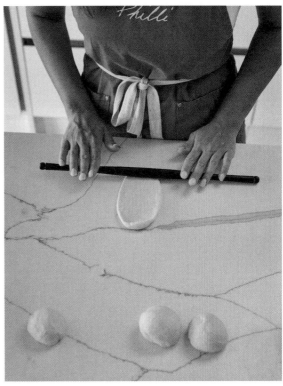

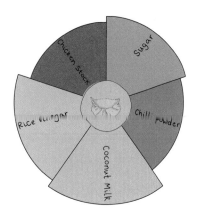

# The Secret Katsu Dunkers

Let me tell you a secret: in many restaurants katsu sauce is made from a curry roux. If you've seen those Japanese curry blocks before, it's the same thing – all you do is add water. I'm going to show you how to make a curry roux, it's the simplest thing. I like to make a big batch, then cool it in a container before portioning the curry roux into blocks and storing them in the freezer. Then, to make a katsu sauce, you simply add it to water and coconut milk.

**SERVES 4**

### Essential Equipment
Wok; saucepan

FOR THE KATSU SAUCE
50g/1½oz butter or coconut oil
2.5cm/1in piece of ginger, minced
1 garlic clove, minced
30g/1oz plain flour
3 tsp ground cumin
¼ tsp ground turmeric
4 tsp ground coriander
¼ tsp ground fenugreek
   (optional)
¼ nutmeg, grated (optional)
½ tsp ground cinnamon
½ tsp chilli powder
400ml/14fl oz chicken stock
   or water
200ml/7fl oz coconut milk,
   shaken
2 carrots, peeled and sliced
   (optional)
1 tbsp rice vinegar
1 tsp sugar
Salt, to taste

FOR THE CHICKEN TENDERS
500g/1lb 1½oz (about 12)
   chicken mini fillets
60g/2oz plain flour
2 eggs, whisked
65g/2oz panko breadcrumbs
15g/½oz cornflakes, crushed
   (optional)
Oil for shallow frying

TO SERVE
My Squishy Bao (p. 140) or
   cooked sushi rice mixed with
   sushi seasoning
Quick Pickled Cucs (p. 161)

### Note
If serving with bao, sushi rice or pickled cucs, make these beforehand.

**1.** To make the sauce, melt the butter in a saucepan over a medium heat. Once it starts to foam, add in ginger and garlic. Fry until fragrant, about 2 minutes.

**2.** Add in the flour and spices to make a roux.

**3.** Slowly add the chicken stock and then the coconut milk and whisk together. Add the chopped carrots (if using) and cook for 20 minutes over a medium heat or until you have a thick curry sauce and the carrots are tender. **Taste and adjust** the sauce to your palate and season with rice vinegar, sugar and salt to your liking.

**4.** Keep the saucepan over a low heat until you're ready to serve.

**5.** To make the chicken tenders, place the flour and eggs in separate bowls. Mix the panko breadcrumbs and cornflakes in a third bowl.

**6.** Coat the chicken mini fillets in flour, then eggs, then bread-crumbs, using one hand for the dry and one hand for the wet to avoid a sticky mess.

**7.** Heat the oil in a deep saucepan and shallow fry the fillets for 2–3 minutes on each side at 160°C, or until golden and fully cooked with an internal temp of over 65°C.

**8.** Serve the dunkers with a bowl of hot katsu sauce with bao or over rice.

**Note**
You could spray the fillets with oil and roast them in a preheated oven at 180°C for 20 minutes, but, let's be honest, they aren't as good.

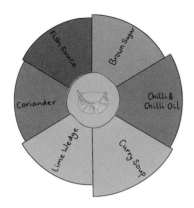

# Khao Soi
## (Northern Chiang Mai Curry Noodles)

I fell in love with khao soi in Chiang Mai as a nineteen-year-old on my first big trip away from home. There was something super comforting about eating this steaming bowl of curry soup noodles in the hills of Northern Thailand. Once I tasted it, I think I must have asked for it in nearly every restaurant we visited that trip – I was hooked. Once you taste this bowl of noods I cannot promise that you won't also become khao soi obsessed.

SERVES 4

### Essential Equipment
Wok or large saucepan; pestle and mortar or small blender

FOR THE KHAO SOI PASTE
4 Thai shallots or 1 banana
    shallot or ¼ red onion, diced
2–6 bird's eye chillies, roughly
    chopped
5cm/2in piece of ginger, roughly
    chopped
1 tbsp shrimp paste (optional)
4 garlic cloves, roughly chopped
½ tsp ground turmeric
1 tbsp ground coriander
1 tsp salt

FOR THE SOUP
300g/10½oz dried egg noodles
100ml/3½fl oz oil
400ml/14fl oz coconut milk
    (1 tin), unshaken
2 lime leaves, fresh or frozen,
    or zest of 1 lime
2 lemongrass sticks, bashed
    to split
4 chicken thigh fillets
½ tbsp garam masala
½ tbsp fish sauce
2 tbsp brown sugar or
    palm sugar
300g/10½oz dried egg noodles

**1.** Blend the paste ingredients with 3 teaspoons of water until the paste reaches a thick consistency.

**2.** Boil the noodles in salted water until just soft, about 10 minutes, and then refresh in cold water. Take one sixth of the noodles and drain through a sieve. Keep the rest of the noodles in a bowl of water until you're ready to serve.

**3.** Heat the oil in a wok or deep saucepan, take the noodles from the sieve and shake, then dry on kitchen paper. Fry the dried noodles for 5 minutes until golden and crisp. Remove and drain on kitchen paper.

Handful of coriander, chopped
1 bird's eye chilli, finely sliced
2 Thai shallots or ¼ red onion,
    sliced
1 lime, wedged
1 tsp Philli's Chilli Oil (p. 250) or
    shop-bought chilli oil

**4.** Remove all but 1 tablespoon of the oil and add 2 tablespoons of coconut fat (the white stuff from the top of the tin). Heat until the fat splits in the pan and then add the curry paste, lime leaves and lemongrass and fry for 1 minute until fragrant.

**5.** Add the rest of the coconut milk and 225ml/8fl oz water and bring the pan to a simmer. Add in the chicken thighs and cook for 20 minutes.

**6.** Once the chicken is fully cooked, remove it from the sauce and shred with a fork. Add the garam masala, fish sauce and brown sugar to the curry soup.

**7.** Divide the noodles among the bowls, pour over the hot soup and chicken and top with fresh coriander, chilli, sliced shallots, lime wedges, chilli oil and crispy noodles. **Taste adjust** to your palate.

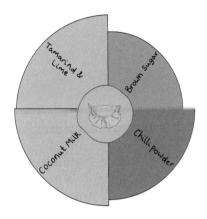

# *Fancy* Short Rib Rendang with Beef Dripping Crispy Potatoes

Rendang is one of Indonesia's most popular curries. It's actually a coconut milk-based dish that is cooked so far down that it splits and becomes a rich, dark curry. There are various different types of rendang, but I love a short rib so here's my version.

SERVES 4

**Essential Equipment**
Small blender or stick blender; large ovenproof pot with lid

FOR THE REMPAH SPICE PASTE
8 small shallots or 2 banana
    shallots
6 garlic cloves
2.5cm/1in piece of galangal
    or 1 tsp galangal paste or
    horseradish
5cm/2in piece of ginger

FOR THE BRAISE
1kg/2lb 3oz beef short rib
1 tsp salt
1 tbsp oil
2 lemongrass sticks
4 lime leaves or skin of 1 lime
2 cardamom pods (optional)
1 star anise (optional)
1 cinnamon stick or 1 tsp ground
    cinnamon
3 tsp ground coriander
1 tsp ground turmeric
4–6 tsp chilli powder
800ml/28fl oz coconut milk
500g/1lb 1½oz baby potatoes,
    halved
1 tbsp brown sugar
1 tbsp tamarind paste
Sprinkle of flaky sea salt

**1.** Preheat the oven to 160°C (140°C fan oven) Gas 3.

**2.** Remove excess fat from the short ribs with a sharp knife so you can just see the marbled meat underneath. Keep the reserved beef trimmings. Flip the rib over and remove the membrane in the back of the bone using a fork to pick off the side and then pulling with a firm grip and a piece of kitchen paper. Carve the ribs into individual bones. Season the beef on all sides with salt and leave to rest on a tray.

**3.** To make the paste, blend the shallots, garlic, galangal and ginger into a smooth paste.

TO SERVE
1 lime, wedged
Crispy Things (optional, p. 252)

HOW TO PREPARE SHORT RIB

**4.** Heat the oil in a large pot over a high heat and sear the beef on all sides, 1 or 2 ribs at a time depending on the size of your pot, then remove and reserve.

**5.** Turn down the heat, add the rempah paste and cook for 2–4 minutes.

**6.** Add the lemongrass, lime leaves, cardamom, star anise and cinnamon stick (if using ground cinnamon wait to add with the rest of the spices), then cook for a further 2 minutes.

**7.** Add the rest of the spices and the coconut milk. Put the beef back in.

**8.** Cover the pot and place in the oven for 4–5 hours, turning the beef every hour.

**9.** After 2½ hours add the fat set aside from the beef trimmings and add to a heavy frying pan, like a cast-iron pan. Place over a medium heat until all the fat has rendered out of the beef trimmings; it'll take about 30 minutes.

**10.** Wash the potatoes and pat dry, then add them to the frying pan and gently crisp for 5–10 minutes. If your frying pan is ovenproof, throw everything in the oven; if not, tip it all into an oven tray and roast for 1 hour.

**11.** Check the beef and make sure it's fork tender. Carefully remove the beef from the pot and allow to rest on an oven tray. Skim off any excess fat from the sauce and discard in a heatproof container.

**12.** Finish the sauce by bringing up to the boil and add in the brown sugar and tamarind paste. **Taste and adjust** to your palate.

**13.** Turn up the oven to 220°C (200°C fan oven) Gas 7.

**14.** When the oven is hot, put the short ribs back in to caramelise for 5–10 minutes.

**15.** Remove the potatoes from the oven and season with flaky salt.

**16.** Serve 1 rib per person. Ladle the sauce over the meat and serve it with lime wedges and Crispy Things and the potatoes to share.

# Mango Crumble and Chai Custard

There's nothing more comforting than a crumble – sweet indulgence at its finest – and pairing it with warming chai spice. I love a cup of chai and for this recipe I make the custard by infusing the milk with beaut chai spices.

SERVES 8

**Essential Equipment**
23 x 33cm / 9 x 13in dish;
hand whisk; sieve

FOR THE FILLING
4 mangoes, about 600g/10½oz, peeled and diced
60g/2½oz sugar
1 tsp ground cinnamon

FOR THE CRUMBLE TOPPING
150g/5oz plain flour
70g/2½oz sugar
½ tsp salt
100g/3½oz butter, at room temperature, diced

FOR THE CHAI CRÈME ANGLAISE (CUSTARD)
300ml/11fl oz whole milk
300ml/11fl oz double cream
1 vanilla pod, split and scraped, or 1 tsp vanilla extract
1 cinnamon stick or ½ tsp ground cinnamon
6 x 5mm/¼in slices of ginger
2 black tea bags
2 star anise (optional)
2 cloves (optional)
2 cardamom pods (optional)
3 egg yolks
6 tbsp sugar

**1.** Preheat the oven to 220°C (200°C fan oven) Gas 6.

**2.** Put the mangoes, sugar, ground cinnamon and 50ml/ 1½fl oz of water in a saucepan and heat for 5 minutes until all the sugar is dissolved. Then place in your oven dish.

**3.** Place the flour, sugar, salt and butter in a bowl and crumble together using the tips of your fingers until all the butter is incorporated and it's a crumbly texture.

**4.** Sprinkle the crumble topping over the mango and cook in the oven for 35–45 minutes or until the topping looks golden and the edges are bubbling.

**5.** Make the chai custard by heating the milk and cream in a saucepan with all the spices and tea bags over a medium-low heat, stirring occasionally, for 20 minutes or until a caramel colour and smelling fragrant.

**6.** Whisk the egg yolks and sugar together in a bowl. Then use a sieve to strain the infused milky cream over the yolks, in three additions, whisking in between.

**7.** Pour the yolk mixture back into the saucepan and whisk while cooking it over a low heat until thickened – it should just coat the back of a spoon. Keep the custard on the lowest setting if serving immediately. If serving later, pour into a heatproof container and cover with cling film so that the film touches the custard, otherwise you'll get a skin.

**8.** Once the crumble topping begins to brown, remove the crumble from the oven and leave to rest for 10 minutes before serving with the hot chai custard.

**Tip**
Don't amend this recipe drastically as it is a dessert recipe; however, you can play around with the fruits in the crumble and the spices in the custard.

TARTY

Tarty is the exclamation mark of flavour which smacks you around the face and lights up your eyes. Tarty flavour is due to the acid in food that literally makes you smile.

Acidity is supposed to tell us to avoid that food. However, there is something exceedingly moreish about a tart flavour. If you've ever seen a child's face wince when they lick a lemon, followed by a huge grin and further chomps on the citrus fruit, you can easily see that tarty flavours are a craving.

Foods taste tart because they contain some form of acid, in which the positively charged hydrogen ions, $H^+$ remove themselves and attach to water. The stronger the acid, the lower pH in a solution on a scale from 14–0. With lemon juice the hydrogen ion detaches really easily from the citric acid.

**A few examples**

- pH 7 – Water (neutral)
- pH 5 – Black coffee
- pH 3 – Orange juice
- pH 1 – Gastric acid
- pH 6 – Urine
- pH 4 – Tomato juice
- pH 2 – Lemon juice

The main acids responsible for Tarty flavours are:

◆ Acetic acid, often found in different kinds of vinegar, rice vinegar and mirin.

◆ Ascorbic acid, or Vit C, found in citrus fruit, peppers, strawberries, blackcurrants, broccoli and Brussels sprouts.

◆ Citric acid, which is found in citrus fruits like lemons, limes, oranges and grapefruits.

◆ Lactic acid, which forms from lactic acid bacteria, and can be found in fermented products like tofu, cheeses and kimchi.

◆ Malic acid, found in tomatoes, apples, bananas and cherries.

◆ Tartaric acid, a key component of tamarind, grapes, apples, apricots, and bananas.

I learned the importance of tarty flavours with one of the first recipes I made in a professional kitchen: a simple mayonnaise. Mayonnaise is an emulsion of egg and oil, commonly combined with mustard, garlic, vinegar and salt. Vinegar is essential as it balances the rich sauce. My head chef always told me to add more vinegar to the mayonnaise, even though I had added half a bottle of vinegar already. I thought it was ridiculous and couldn't possibly add any more; however, when I tasted the sauce, the acidity heightened the other flavours, and the sauce was balanced. I still use this learning today. Always taste a dish to make sure you have a slight squeeze just behind your ears at the end of your jawline; you can literally feel when you have the flavour just right. My theory is that the hydrogen ion released from the acid is very reactive so that it pairs with bases (OH-) easily to form water. This is why the acidity lessens when you heat lemon juice in food and when you leave it for a long time, like a leftover curry after a night in the fridge. As a general rule I tend to add acid right at the end of the cooking to heighten the acid flavour and check for acidity last.

IF YOU'VE EVER SEEN A CHILD'S FACE WINCE WHEN THEY LICK A LEMON, FOLLOWED BY A HUGE GRIN AND FURTHER CHOMPS ON THE CITRUS FRUIT, YOU CAN EASILY SEE THAT TARTY FLAVOURS ARE A CRAVING.

I feel that high acid dishes cool the body when in a hot, humid climate. These dishes lend themselves to the summer months when you're looking for something a little lighter. We'll be cooking South Indian-style curries, sour Filipino-inspired dishes and some banging fresh desserts. Once you start to incorporate Tarty flavours into your cooking, it'll be an addictive craving that you come back to time and time again.

## Tarty ingredients

- Chinese black vinegar
- Yuzu
- Sake
- Lemongrass
- Rice vinegar
- Tamarind
- Limes
- Tomatoes
- White vinegar
- Shaoxing wine
- Lemons
- Kimchi

# Disco Pickles (Ve)

I believe that you should always have a jar of pickles at the back of your fridge. They add great colour, depth and, most importantly, sharpness to a dish. I've based these pickle recipes on a classic, and all you need to remember is the ratio *3 water: 2 vinegar: 1 sugar*. You can then start playing and getting creative with different herbs and spices, vinegars and sugars to add complexity with flavour. The beauty of these pickles is that you can make them and leave them at the back of your fridge for a couple of weeks as you add them to salads, rice dishes, sandwiches or anything that calls for an extra little sharp hit.

I munched pickles throughout Japan (where they're known as tsukemono, Japanese-style pickles), South Korea and China, and I've based these recipes on some of my faves I came across my journey.

## Pickled Shrooms

Pickled shrooms are a staple in my fridge; when I worked at Gordon Ramsay's restaurants, these were often used to garnish dishes. I then tried David Chang's recipe of pickled, dried shitake mushrooms; these mushrooms can literally be added to any dish. Pickled mushrooms have a little punch of sharpness and give a beaut umami flavour that we all crave.

**Essential Equipment**
2 jam jars, sterilised

300ml/11fl oz water
200ml/7fl oz rice vinegar
100g/3½oz sugar
50g/1½oz dried shitake
   mushrooms or 2 packs shimeji
   (the tiny brown or white
   mushrooms)

**1.** Bring the water, vinegar and sugar to the boil in a saucepan, stirring to make sure you dissolve all the sugar.

**2.** Grab a glass jam jar, and if you're using the shimeji shrooms snip off the tops of the mushrooms to about 4cm/1½in long using kitchen scissors. If you're using shitakes, just pop them straight in the jars.

**3.** Take the pickle juice off the heat and allow it to come back down to room temp, then pour the juice over the shrooms, making sure everything is covered.

**4.** Seal the jars, place in your fridge, leave for a day, then start munching your way through and adding to your favourite salads.

**5.** These mushrooms will keep for up to a month.

**Tip**
Look out for the whole dried shitake mushrooms in specialist shops: pickle whole and slice thinly to garnish your dish.

Don't throw away the pickle juice; use this to make a delicious salad dressing.

# Korean-Inspired Yellow Pickled Radish
## (Danmuji)

Once you pickle a radish, it removes the spicy flavour, leaving you with delicious sweetness. Adding a touch of turmeric to the liquor makes the vegetable a bright golden colour. If you're into fermented flavour, you'll love this one. However, this comes with a warning as if you leave it too long, it takes on a beautiful funky taste. For optimal results, pickle for up to 4 days.

**Essential Equipment**
2 jam jars, sterilised

300ml/11fl oz water
200ml/7fl oz rice vinegar
100g/3½oz sugar
½ tsp ground turmeric
1 large daikon radish (mooli),
    cut into 2.5cm/1in matchsticks,
    or 200g/7oz radishes, washed
    and quartered

**1.** Bring the water, vinegar, sugar and turmeric to the boil in a saucepan, stirring to make sure you dissolve all the sugar.

**2.** Remove the saucepan from the heat and let the liquid come back to room temperature.

**3.** Pack the radish tightly into the glass jars.

**4.** Fill the jars with the pickle liquor and make sure all the radish is covered.

**5.** Seal the jars and keep in the fridge.

# Pink Pickled Shallots

These are a chef's favourite: they add bright pink colour, and the trick to get them super deep pink is to use fresh beetroot and leave the shallots overnight.

**Essential Equipment**
2 jam jars, sterilised

½ tsp yellow mustard seeds
    (optional)
300ml/11fl oz water
200ml/7fl oz rice vinegar
100g/3½oz sugar
½ fresh beetroot, sliced
5 banana shallots, peeled,
    sliced in 2cm/¾in rounds

**1.** If you're using mustard seeds, gently toast them in a saucepan over a low heat to release their aroma for 30 seconds.

**2.** Bring the water, rice vinegar, sugar and beetroot to the boil in a saucepan, making sure the sugar dissolves completely.

**3.** Take the pan off the heat and allow the pickle juice to cool to room temperature.

**4.** Pack the sliced shallots into the jars and pour over the pickle juice.

**5.** Seal the jars and allow everything to marinate overnight.

**6.** You can nibble at these pickles for up to a month.

### Tip
These pickles are great on salads and for garnishing tartare. When you remove the shallots from the jar, make sure you drain them on a piece of kitchen paper to stop the pickles from 'bleeding' on the plate.

# Pickled Chilli

If you're into spice but don't want to blow your head off completely, pickled chillies are the perfect garnish. The acidity and sweetness of the pickle reduce the spiciness of the chilli peppers.

**Essential Equipment**
2 jam jars, sterilised

300ml/11fl oz water
200ml/7fl oz rice vinegar
100g/3½oz sugar
20 red chillies, sliced into
   1cm rounds

**1.** Whack the water, rice vinegar and sugar into a saucepan. Cook over a medium heat until all the sugar dissolves and the liquid boils.

**2.** Take off the heat and allow everything to cool to room temperature.

**3.** Pack the sliced chillies into a jar and pour over the cooled pickle juice.

**4.** Allow to pickle overnight and enjoy them for up to a month.

# Quick Pickled Cucs

If you don't have the time to wait for pickles overnight or, like me, you forgot, cucs are your bestie. You can slice and mix, and they only take 20 minutes. Perfect for a last-minute garnish.

**Essential Equipment**
2 jam jars, sterilised

½ cucumber, sliced as thin
   as you can
4 tbsp rice vinegar or white
   wine vinegar
1 tbsp sugar
Pinch of salt

**1.** Mix all your ingredients and marinate for 20 minutes. The cucumber will lightly pickle and soften.

**Tip**
Use a mandoline to get evenly cut cucumber without pro chef skills. Just make sure you're careful and use the guard, as the blade is super sharp, and you can cut yourself easily.

# How I Kimchi

In South Korean cuisine, kimchi is a palate cleanser as well as an ingredient; when you're too full to eat another bite, grab a mouthful of kimchi. Kimchi is my favourite of all the fermented varieties of cabbage-type things. South Koreans have got it right.

You can now find kimchi in your local supermarket. However, it's satisfying seeing a vegetable transform over time and create a beautiful fermentation.

All fermentations are essentially a four-stage process: chop, salt, pack and wait. Fermentations vary depending on the ingredients you're using; however, they are all linked by this same process. Within the kimchi realm, it's not only limited to cabbage; you can get radish kimchi, cucumber kimchi and even fish entrails kimchi, which I have tried.

MAKES 1 LARGE JAR

**Essential Equipment**
Large glass jar; gloves

1 napa cabbage (commonly called Chinese leaf), about 600g/1lb 5oz
50g/1½ oz salt
1 tbsp glutinous rice flour
½ tbsp sugar
3 tbsp gochugaru (Korean chilli powder) or Chinese chilli powder
1 tbsp shrimp paste or fish sauce (optional)
2.5cm/1in piece of ginger, minced
2 garlic cloves, minced
3 spring onions, sliced
1 pear, shredded thinly
½ carrot, shredded thinly
½ daikon, shredded thinly

**1.** Grab your cabbage and peel off the outer leaves. Discard these, quarter the cabbage and then make sure to wash in between the layers of the vegetable. There are often little bits of dirt between the leaves. Dice the cabbage into large chunks.

**2.** Take a large bowl and generously rub in the salt to season the cabbage, smushing the salt and squeezing the leaves (don't worry about the amount of salt, we'll be washing it off later). Leave the cabbage in the bowl for 3–5 hours, mixing every hour. You'll notice that all the water comes out of the cabbage and you'll get a pool of water at the bottom of the bowl.

**3.** Put your rice flour and sugar in a saucepan with 130ml/4½fl oz water, and cook over a medium heat for 10 minutes until thickened. Then add in the gochugaru, shrimp paste, ginger and garlic and mix into a paste.

**4.** Wash the wilted cabbage, then drain, squeezing out as much water as possible. Glove up, and start coating the cabbage in the chilli paste, getting in all the nooks and crannies.

**5.** Add in the spring onion, pear, carrot and daikon and give everything a good mix.

**6.** Get yourself a Kilner jar (if you want to be edgy) or a couple of leftover sterilised jam jars. Tightly pack the veg into the jar, making sure there are no air gaps.

**7.** Fill a ziplock bag with weighted stones, coins or dried rice and use this heavy bag to weigh down the cabbage. It's super important to keep the cabbage below the liquid, otherwise the ferment might get mouldy.

**8.** Seal up your jar and leave it for 2 days, and then open the jar. You should start to see bubbles rising in the liquid; this means everything is working! Leave your jar for an additional 1–5 days, opening (or burping) every day. Keep smelling and tasting your fermented juice, and once you get to the desired funk, remove your weighted bag and pop the jar in the fridge. You can enjoy the kimchi for up to a month in the fridge: add it to a cheese toastie, Korean Fried Chicken Burgers (p. 64) or Korean-Inspired Spicy Cheesy Rice Cakes (p. 82).

## Troubleshoot

*White or light-yellow mould* = remove the mould with a stainless steel spoon and discard it; remove any veggies around the mould as well.

*Coloured mould* = this mould has been left a while, and you could remove it; however, this might have penetrated deeper into the ferment, and you may need to cut your losses and start again.

*No bubbles* = move it to a sterilised, airtight jar and leave it for a little longer. Patience is key with fermentations; it could be too much salt or a cooler temperature hindering the fermentation.

## Science things

The first step is to draw out the water from the cabbage via osmosis by adding the salt; this also helps preserve the kimchi and stops unwanted bacteria from growing. The fermentation is a lactic acid bacterium (LAB). It grows under anaerobic conditions, which means you should keep the kimchi under the solution and away from the air to stop other unwanted bacteria from growing.

The rice starch and LAB kick-start the fermentation of the cabbage. The natural fermentation sugars in the kimchi are converted to lactic acid, decreasing the pH, making the kimchi taste sourer over time.

Optimal fermentation conditions for kimchi are 3 days at 20°C, 3 per cent salt.

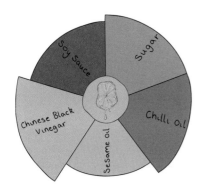

# Smacked Sichuan Pepper and Black Vinegar Cucumber (Ve)

This dish is an ideal side for any dining table or served as a lighter option for nibbles before a dinner party – it will satisfy any guest. Or you could have it as a guilt-free, late-night Scooby snack. If you want to relieve a bit of stress, it is great to get the rolling pin out and whack a cuc. The cuc will break irregularly, meaning all that delish marinade will soak into all the nooks and crannies of the cucumber. It's also ready in under 30 minutes, a no-brainer.

SERVES 4

## Essential Equipment
Rolling pin; pestle and mortar

1 large Persian cucumber
   or 1 normal cucumber
1 tsp salt
½ tsp Sichuan peppercorns
   (optional)
1 garlic clove, minced
1 tbsp sugar
2 tsp soy sauce
4 tbsp Chinese black vinegar
   (Chinkiang) or white rice
   vinegar
1 tsp sesame oil
1 tbsp Philli's Chilli Oil (p. 250)
   or ¼–½ tbsp shop-bought
   chilli oil
Pinch of mixed sesame seeds

**1.** Trim off the top and bottom tips of the cucumber and, using a clean rolling pin, start whacking the cucumber until it cracks.

**2.** Using your knife, quarter the cucumber lengthwise and chunk it up into bite-size pieces.

**3.** Put the cucumber in a bowl and sprinkle on the salt, making sure you coat all the cucumber. Leave it for 30 minutes while you make the dressing.

**4.** Crack the Sichuan peppercorns in a pestle and mortar and whisk with the garlic, sugar, soy sauce, Chinese black vinegar, sesame oil and chilli oil for the dressing.

**Taste adjust**: the sauce is super sharp but balanced with garlic and chilli. If you want to reduce the sharpness add a pinch more sugar.

**5.** Remove the cucumber from the salt and drain on kitchen paper.

**6.** Pile the cucumber on your serving plate, drizzle on the vinegar dressing, and garnish with sesame seeds – because they look beaut.

### Tip
Don't obliterate your cucumber too much or you'll end up with cucumber pulp, but you do need to make sure the cucumber splits, or you'll have to marinate it in salt for longer. If you don't have a rolling pin, use the flat blade of a knife

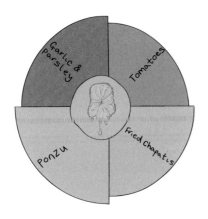

# Citrus Marinated Tomatoes with Garlicky Oil and Crispy Chapatis

This dish is great for sharing. Think of it as the love child of a panzanella salad, sexy tomato nachos and bruschetta. The quality of the tomato really makes this dish; they're at their best from mid to late summer. I love a large beef tomato or smaller sweeter cherry tomatoes.

If you want to prepare beforehand, you can leave the ponzu, tomatoes and garlic dressing separately for up to 3 days, and they'll keep improving. All you need to do to serve is toast off some crispy chapatis, mix everything together and, boom, you're done.

SERVES 2–3 AS A STARTER

**Essential Equipment**
Small ovenproof dish or saucepan

60ml/2fl oz olive oil
5 garlic cloves, thinly sliced
3 large beef tomatoes or 300g/10½oz cherry tomatoes
Pinch of salt
4 tbsp Ponzu (p. 253, or use shop-bought)
Handful of parsley
100–200ml/3½–7fl oz neutral oil for shallow frying
4 My Mum's Chapatis (p. 116), or shop-bought or tortilla wraps

**1.** Preheat the oven to 140°C (120°C fan oven) Gas 1.

**2.** Pour all the olive oil into a small ovenproof saucepan or dish and add in the sliced garlic. Make sure all the garlic is submerged in the oil and cook in the oven for 30 minutes.

**3.** Slice the tomatoes down the cross-section of the tomato (it looks way nicer) and put them in a bowl with a good pinch of salt. Make sure all the tomatoes are coated and leave them for 30 minutes.

**4.** Take your ponzu dressing and strain over the tomatoes, removing the citrus peel and kombu. Allow everything to marinate.

**5.** Take the confit garlic oil out of the oven and leave it to come back to room temperature.

**6.** Once the garlicky oil is cool enough to touch, finely chop a large handful of parsley and mix through the oil.

**7.** Before serving, heat a large frying pan with a couple of centimetres of neutral oil and chop the chapatis into 5cm/2in triangles. Fry off the chapatis until crisp. Make sure to work in batches and not overcrowd the pan. Remove the crispy chapatis with a slotted spoon and drain on kitchen paper. Season with salt.

**8.** Mix the chapatis with the tomatoes – the dressing will slightly soak into the crispy bread – and then drizzle over the garlicky parsley oil.

**Taste and adjust** as you eat.

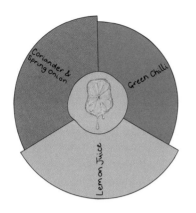

# Gunpowder Pots

Okay, so you might think it's weird to squeeze lemon over potatoes. However, can I please draw your attention to salt and vinegar crisps? These gunpowder pots are sour, salty and definitely spicy. They are now a staple in my kitchen, and if you're feeling lazy this seasoning is a great way to jazz up your oven chips.

SERVES 4 AS A SIDE

**Essential Equipment**
Large oven tray

600g/1lb 5oz baby new potatoes, halved
1 tsp cumin seeds
1 tsp fennel seeds (optional)
½ tsp ground coriander
¼ tsp ground turmeric
½ tsp salt
1 tbsp neutral oil
4 green rocket chillies or 2 large green chillies, finely sliced
6 spring onions, finely sliced
½ handful fresh coriander leaves, chopped
Juice of ½ lemon

**1.** Preheat the oven to 200°C (180°C fan oven) Gas 6.

**2.** Slice the potatoes in half and boil in salted water for 12–15 minutes.

**3.** Mix the cumin seeds, fennel seeds, coriander, turmeric, salt and vegetable oil in a large bowl.

**4.** Once the potatoes are just soft, strain them through a colander then add to the mixed spices and tumble all the ingredients together.

**5.** Spread the potatoes on an oven tray and place them in the oven for 20–25 minutes.

**6.** Once crisp, take out of the oven and serve in a bowl, sprinkled with green chilli, spring onion, fresh coriander and a good squeeze of lemon juice.

**Taste and adjust** as you eat.

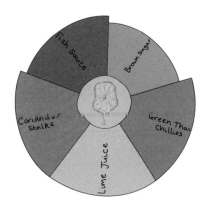

# Crispy Tofu Nuggz and Green Nam Jim (Ve)

I think it's fair to say we all love nuggz, but sometimes you want something a little lighter than your classic Maccy D's. These nuggz are almost as quick to make as the time it takes you to order to your door, and you'll feel a lot better after eating them. I nearly forgot about the sauce. It's super yum – make sure you have loads of limes to hand because you want it sour.

SERVES 4 AS A MAIN OR
8 SNACKS / MAKES 16 NUGGZ

**Essential Equipment**
Blender or pestle and mortar

2 blocks smoked tofu (approx.
    500g/1lb 1½oz)
16 sheets Vietnamese rice paper
    (about 1 pack)
50g/1½oz cornflour
200–400ml/7–14fl oz neutral oil,
    for frying
Green Nam Jim (p. 254)
Handful of fresh coriander

TO SERVE
Blanched vermicelli rice noodles
    or jasmine rice if serving as
    a main

**1.** Make the Green Nam Jim prior to beginning the recipe as well as the rice or noodles if serving as a main meal.

**2.** Cut the tofu into 5 x 2.5cm/ 2 x 1in squares, 8 pieces per block of tofu. Fill a bowl with water and dunk the rice paper into the water quickly, then lay it on a chopping board. Place a square of tofu onto the rice paper, which should be just softened, and fold the rice paper like an envelope around the tofu. Then add to a well-oiled plate while you complete the rest of your nuggz.

**3.** To cook your nuggz, heat a wok or large frying pan with 5cm/2in of oil. Just before adding your nuggz, coat them in cornflour and then shallow fry the tofu parcels in the oil for 3 minutes on each side until golden and crisp. Remove from the oil with a slotted spoon and drain on kitchen paper.

**4.** Dunk a tofu nug into the sauce, **taste and adjust** the sauce to your profile.

**5.** Serve the nuggz with the Green Nam Jim and a sprinkle of chopped coriander.

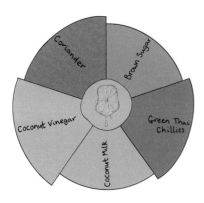

# Sea Bass Filipino-Inspired Kinilaw

Kinilaw is a bit like ceviche, but the main difference is it's got loads of coconut creaminess as well. I lapped this up on the beaches in Cebu. However, I've changed it up slightly as you usually find this dish well marinated so the fish almost cooks in the vinegar. I love the raw fish style, so I've added the dressing right at the end just before you serve it. As it is served raw, make sure to buy your fish from your local monger so that it is very fresh.

SERVES 3–4 AS A STARTER

### Essential Equipment
Super sharp knife, whisk or blender

2 sea bass fillets, skinned and pin boned, about 300g/10½oz
2 tbsp calamansi juice or 1–2 limes, juiced
3 tbsp coconut vinegar or 2 tbsp white malt vinegar
4 tbsp coconut milk, shaken
2.5cm/1in piece of ginger, minced
¼ small red onion, super finely diced
1½ tbsp light brown sugar or palm sugar
Handful of coriander, chopped
2–4 Thai chillies, sliced
50g/1½oz chicharron (optional)

**1.** Ask your local fish counter for fresh sea bass, and to remove the skin and pin bone the fish.

**2.** Place the fish in the freezer for 10–20 minutes to firm up while you make the dressing.

**3.** Stick blend or whisk together the calamansi juice, coconut vinegar and coconut milk, making sure there are no lumps. Stir through the ginger, red onion and brown sugar.

**4.** Take the fish out from the freezer: it should be firm to touch but not frozen. Dice the fillets into 2cm/¾in cubes.

**5.** Before serving, add the dressing to the diced fish along with half the coriander and chillies. Mix everything and **taste and adjust** to your palate. Leave for 2½ minutes.

**6.** Serve onto plates and garnish with the rest of the coriander, chillies and chicharron, if using.

### Tip
You can prepare this ahead of time. Simply stop after slicing your fish, cover and leave in the fridge. Make the dressing and keep separately, then mix with the fish when you are ready to serve.

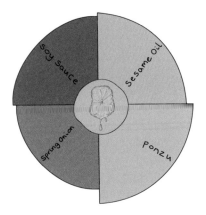

# *Fancy* Tuna Tataki with Gomae Dressing

Tuna tataki was one of the first dishes that made me fall in love with Japanese flavours – great tuna with a beautiful citrus sauce, it's all simplicity and elegance. You can now find sashimi-grade tuna more readily, so why not give this one a go?

When I was in Tokyo, I visited the famous Tsukiji market where the tuna auction is held at around 4am. The tuna is prepared into different cuts just before the chefs enter the market to get the best quality fish for Tokyo's top restaurants.

SERVES 4 AS A STARTER

**Essential Equipment**
Super sharp knife

400g/14oz sashimi-grade tuna
1 tbsp neutral oil
1 spring onion, sliced
Sprinkle of sesame seeds

FOR THE TATAKI SAUCE
1 spring onion, thinly sliced
1.5cm/½in piece of ginger, minced
3 tsp sesame oil
1.5 tbsp soy sauce or tamari
4 tbsp Ponzu (p. 253) or use shop-bought

FOR THE GOMAE
3 tbsp tahini or sesame paste
Juice of ½ lemon
1 tbsp soy sauce or tamari
½ tsp honey

HOW TO SHARPEN YOUR KNIFE

SLICING TUNA

**1.** Rub the fish with the oil and lightly sear the tuna on all sides in a non-stick pan over a high heat. Remove from the pan and allow the tuna to rest in the fridge.

**2.** To make the tataki dressing, whisk together all the ingredients for the sauce. **Taste and adjust** as you eat.

**3.** For the gomae dressing, mix the tahini, lemon juice, soy sauce and honey with a spoon or mini-whisk. You'll see the tahini start to break and split like sand; this is correct. Gradually spoon in 1 teaspoon of water at a time until you get a thick yoghurt consistency.

**4.** Take the tuna out of the fridge and get your sharpest, longest knife. I find it easiest to cut the loin in half then half again, and then again until you have 8 equal pieces. For each slice make one even stroke rather than a sawing motion.

**5.** Spoon the gomae dressing onto a plate and spread out with the back of your spoon. Layer the tuna onto the plate and serve the tataki dressing as a dipping sauce. Garnish with thinly sliced spring onion and sesame seeds.

**Note**
Sashimi tuna is kept at -60°C and frozen on the boat to kill bacteria and keep the fish texture.

You can prepare a whole tuna into different cuts like any meat. The belly has a different texture to the loin, like a pork belly and loin are very different. The main types are:

◆ Otoro – fatty tuna belly (most prized tuna)

◆ Chutoro – medium fatty tuna

◆ Akami – lean tuna loin (recommended for this dish)

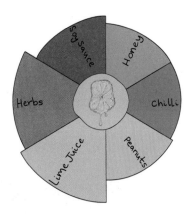

# Tamarind and Lime Glazed Salmon

SERVES 4

**Essential Equipment**
Oven tray

1 Thai chilli, green or red,
   finely sliced
4 tbsp honey
6 tbsp soy sauce
1 tbsp fish sauce (optional)
2 garlic cloves, minced
5cm/2in piece of ginger, minced
4 x 200g/7oz salmon fillets
50g/1½oz tamarind paste,
   or juice of 1 lime and
   1 tbsp honey
Juice of 2 limes
Small handful of mint and
   coriander, chopped
2 tbsp roasted peanuts, chopped

TO SERVE
This goes great with Fennel and
   Cucumber Slaw (p. 196) and a
   cold glass of rosé.

Eating fresh tamarind is an experience like no other. The seeds are super tart with naturally occurring tartaric acid (cream of tartar). This tangy flavour works beautifully with the fatty salmon. Fresh tamarind and tamarind concentrate are hard to come by in the supermarket, but if you have tamarind concentrate it's more acidic so halve the quantity in the recipe. You'll probably be able to find tamarind paste and tamarind sauce – please, please, please stay away from the sauce and pick up the paste. The sauce contains more sugar; the paste is straight blended tamarind, which is what we'll be using in this recipe.

**This is the perfect dish to wow guests at a dinner party, it'll look and taste *mega*.**

**1.** Mix the chilli, honey, soy sauce, fish sauce, garlic and ginger together and taste.

**2.** Line a deep oven tray with baking parchment and place the salmon skin side down. Pour the dressing over the salmon and marinate at room temperature for between 20 and 30 minutes.

**3.** When you're ready to cook, preheat the oven to 230°C (210°C fan oven) Gas 8 and place the tray in the oven for 9–12 minutes, until it reaches an internal temperature of 45–50°C. The fish will take on a deep caramel colour and it will start to smell super fragrant. Take out the fish and mix together the tamarind and lime juice. Glaze the fish with the tamarind dressing. Cover in loads of herbs and peanuts.

**Taste and adjust** as you eat; if you want more sourness, add lime.

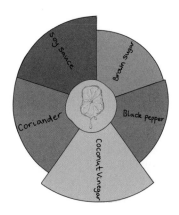

# Filipino-Inspired Chicken Adobo

This is my version of chicken adobo, a Filipino national dish, which is sour and has loads of soy. The sauce is a balance of soy sauce, vinegar, black pepper and sugar, all simple ingredients that you can whip together very quickly. The sauce becomes super sticky; it's not slow-cooked, but you wouldn't believe it wasn't. You can cheat your way to flavour with this recipe.

SERVES 4

**Essential Equipment**
Large, heavy-based saucepan

½ tbsp neutral oil
8 chicken thighs, skin on
A pinch of salt
2 white onions, sliced
3 garlic cloves, minced
3 tbsp soy sauce
3 bay leaves
12 black peppercorns
100ml/3½fl oz coconut vinegar
    or apple cider vinegar
1 tsp brown sugar
1 tbsp cornflour
Handful of coriander, chopped
2 spring onions, finely sliced

**1.** Heat the oil in a large, heavy-based saucepan over a medium heat. Sprinkle the chicken thighs with salt and sear, skin side down, for 10–12 minutes. Once the skin is crisp remove the thighs and set aside, skin side up. Discard any remaining oil rendered from the chicken thighs, leaving about a tablespoon in the pan.

**2.** Add the onions and allow to caramelise for a further 5 minutes. Place the chicken back in the pan and add 150–300ml/5½–11fl oz water, or until it's just below the chicken skin.

**3.** Add the garlic, soy sauce, bay leaves and black peppercorns and simmer uncovered for 30 minutes until the chicken is softened.

**4.** Add the coconut vinegar and allow it to boil over a high heat for 10 minutes. Add the brown sugar and stir.

**5.** Make sure the chicken is completely cooked and the internal temperature is above 80°C, then remove it from the pan and place onto your serving plate.

**6.** Mix the cornflour with 3 tablespoons of cold water. Add to the sauce and stir to thicken; you want it to coat the back of a spoon. **Taste and adjust** the sauce to your palate.

**7.** Pour the sauce around the chicken (not on the skin) and garnish with coriander and spring onions. Serve with jasmine rice.

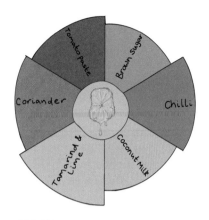

# *Fancy* Goan-Inspired Prawn and Crab Curry with Blistered Tomatoes

This recipe reminds me of my earliest childhood memories in Goa on a beach, snacking on crabs and drinking coconut water. I've made this a little fancy and broken the recipe down, but it still stays true to the heart of the Goan fish curry. The rich brown crab meat combines with coconut milk, balanced beautifully with tamarind paste.

SERVES 4

**Essential Equipment**
Blender or stick blender

FOR THE MASALA PASTE
1 tsp ground cumin
½ tbsp ground coriander
½ tsp ground turmeric
1 tbsp Kashmiri chilli powder or
   2 tbsp smoked paprika and
   1 tsp hot chilli powder
½ tsp salt
6 plump garlic cloves, peeled
   and chopped
4cm/1½in piece of fresh ginger,
   minced

FOR THE CURRY
3 tbsp neutral oil
1 tsp black mustard seeds
Small handful of curry leaves,
   about 15 (optional)
½ red onion, finely sliced
½ tbsp tomato paste
200g/7oz chopped tinned
   tomatoes
400ml/14fl oz coconut milk
100g/3½oz 50:50 fresh brown
   and white crab mix
20 cherry tomatoes
Pinch of salt
Juice of ½ lime
1 tbsp tamarind paste or
   1 lime, juiced

1 tbsp brown sugar or jaggery
450–500g/1lb–1lb 1½oz tiger or
   king prawns, raw, defrosted,
   peeled and deveined
2 large handfuls of coriander
   leaves, chopped
2 green chillies, finely sliced
   (optional)

TO SERVE
Goes great with Green Coconut
   Chutney (p. 254), BBBR (Brown
   Butter Basmati Rice) (p. 130) or
   My Mum's Chapatis (p. 116)

DE-POOPING PRAWNS

1. To make the curry, heat 2 tablespoons of the oil in a large frying pan with a lid. Add a couple of mustard seeds to check if the oil is hot (the seeds will pop and sizzle.) If it's not hot enough, wait a couple of minutes and try again.

2. Add the mustard seeds, cover with the lid, wait until they pop for 10 seconds, add the curry leaves and red onion. Turn down the heat to medium, cover and allow them to caramelise for about 10 minutes while you make the masala paste.

3. Place all the masala paste ingredients and 3 tablespoons of water in a small blender or tall jug with a stick blender. Blitz on high for 5–10 seconds until you have a smooth paste. Add more water if needed to make sure everything is puréed.

4. Add the paste to the onions and curry leaves and cook for 2–3 minutes.

5. Turn up the heat, add the tomato paste and tinned tomatoes, and cook for 3 minutes.

6. Add the coconut milk, 100ml/3½fl oz water and the brown crab meat and simmer over a medium–low heat for 10–15 minutes, uncovered. The rich coconut fat should slightly split out of the sauce. Stir the sauce every so often to make sure it's not catching.

**7.** Heat a frying pan to smoking hot, add 1 tablespoon of oil and the cherry tomatoes and cook until they're blistered. (If you have a blow torch burn the tomato skins on a baking tray.)

**8.** Mix the white crab meat with salt and lime juice.

**9.** Cook the curry sauce until it becomes a deep, rich colour, add the tamarind paste, brown sugar, prawns and blistered cherry tomatoes and cook for 5 minutes.

**10.** Stir in half the coriander and **taste adjust**, then turn off the heat. Then serve up the curry into bowls. Top with a spoon of the white crab meat and garnish with more coriander and sliced green chillies.

# Fuss-Free Yuzu Lemon Tart(ish) with Sichuan Poached Rhubarb

For anyone who's made a lemon tart, you will know it takes a lot of effort, and there's always the chance of a soggy bottom, tough pastry, cracked filling – the list goes on. Let's avoid the risk and make a dish with just as much flavour but that is 100 per cent easier to make. This recipe uses rhubarb; however, rhubarb is not available year-round, so if the calendar is against you fear not, there are many other fruits that you can substitute. You will have to taste the fruit and adjust once cooked, either adding a further spoonful of sugar or a squeeze of lemon juice to the poaching liquor.

SERVES 6

**Essential Equipment**
Whisk or electric whisk

FOR THE WHIPPED YUZU
LEMON CURD
2 gelatine leaves
2 lemons, zest and juice
   (about 5 tbsp juice)
2½ tbsp yuzu juice or 1 more
   lemon, zest and juice
210g/7½oz caster sugar
160g/5½oz butter
4 eggs
165ml/5½fl oz double cream

FOR THE POACHED RHUBARB
50g/1½oz sugar
10 Sichuan peppercorns
3 sticks of rhubarb, cut into
   5cm/2in lengths

FOR THE ALMOND CRUMBLE
70g/2½oz flour
45g/1½oz sugar
40g/1½oz softened butter, diced
20g/½oz cornflakes
30g/1oz flaked almonds
OR
10 amaretti biscuits

**1.** Soak the gelatine in a little iced water.

**2.** Put the lemon and yuzu juice, zest, sugar and butter in a small saucepan and heat over a low heat until dissolved.

**3.** Whisk the eggs in a separate bowl.

**4.** Pour the sugary, buttery citrus mixture over the eggs and whisk together. Pour back into the saucepan and heat over a medium heat until thickened. You want it to be super thick at a temperature of 83°C.

**5.** Remove the saucepan from the heat. Squeeze out the gelatine from the water and dissolve into the mix. Add the double cream and mix through. Strain through a sieve into a container, using the back of a ladle to push through the liquid.

Cover the surface with cling film. Once cooled to room temperature, chill in the fridge for at least 6 hours and up to 3 days.

**6.** To poach the rhubarb, add the sugar and peppercorns to 100ml/3½fl oz water in a small saucepan and bring to the boil.

**7.** Turn down the heat of the syrup, put the rhubarb in a heatproof container, pour over the hot syrup and leave to cool. If you cover and leave the rhubarb overnight in the fridge it improves the colour and flavour.

**8.** To make the crumble, preheat the oven to 180°C (160°C fan oven) Gas 4.

**9.** Mix the flour and sugar together, then work the butter into the flour mix with your fingertips until you form a crumble. Then fold in the cornflakes and almonds.

**10.** Spread the mix on a baking sheet and bake for 40 minutes, mixing every 8 minutes until golden. Allow to cool to room temperature.

**11.** When you are ready to serve, whip the lemon curd until thick and creamy. (If it's a little runny stick it back in the fridge to firm up for 10 minutes or if it's too stiff add a little extra double cream.) Spoon the whipped curd into a bowl, add the crumble and rhubarb and serve.

**Taste adjust**
This is a dessert recipe so I wouldn't change the ratios drastically however you can play around with different fruits at different times of the year.

SEASONALITY OF SHARP BRITISH FRUIT
*Rhubarb* – late winter and early spring

*Peaches/gooseberries* – mid-summer

*Strawberries/cherries* – summer

*Pears/blackberries* – autumn/winter

# REFINED

I see refined as more of an acquired taste; it's complex and is super useful in cooking to balance dishes. As we refine our palates we grow to love herby and bitter flavours and together in these next recipes we'll explore how to showcase these diverse tastes.

Bitterness isn't always pleasant for us, because throughout evolution a bitter flavour has warned us that certain foods contained toxins. However, a touch of bitterness is great for creating more depth to a dish – think adding a little dark choc to your chilli con carne, or beer to a stew.

A liking for bitterness is generally acquired with age. Back in our cave-dwelling times, the older individuals would eat food they didn't have to compete for as much and would tolerate bitter flavours that were not eaten by the younger stronger beings.

Compounds with alkaline properties often have a bitter taste, like tonic water. Bitter flavour compounds are used in various studies to test for supertasters. If you're really averse to bitter flavours, you might be a supertaster! However, don't worry if you love bitter flavours – as you probably do if you're reading this chapter – as this can mean you enjoy healthier foods and avoid sweet treats.

## A TOUCH OF BITTERNESS IS GREAT FOR CREATING MORE DEPTH TO A DISH – THINK ADDING A LITTLE DARK CHOC TO YOUR CHILLI CON CARNE, OR BEER TO A STEW.

Bitter flavours are often balanced with fat and sugar – think of dark chocolate versus milk in a hot chocolate or espresso versus salted caramel latte. Those are extreme examples, but you get the point. But bitter taste is most effectively balanced with salt. If you fancy a science experiment, grab two glasses of tonic water and salt one. The tonic actually has a lot of sweetness and the salt neutralises its bitterness to produce a sweeter flavour.

This chapter also tackles herbs, and how they are used across Asia to impart a glorious range of different flavour notes to a dish. In Vietnam and Thailand, I love it when, alongside the condiments, a full basket of herbs is placed in the centre of the table for you to season your dish to your preference. The herbs found in different regions vary massively, and many of the herbs used are hard to find in your local supermarket. Those you can find are often flown in, so I've tried to swap in where possible just so we keep our carbon footprint down.

A top tip that many chefs practise in restaurants to extend the shelf life of their fresh herbs: simply use a damp J-cloth or kitchen paper lightly rolled around a bunch of herbs. This will double their shelf life in the fridge.

Whether it's a pork larb, green curry mussels or a super dark choc pud, I hope you'll see that bitter and herby is beautiful.

**Refined ingredients**

- *Herbs:*
  Coriander
  Thai basil
  Holy basil
  Chives
  Spring onion
  Parsley
  Garlic chives
  Mint
  Curry leaves
  Shiso/Perilla leaves
  Betel leaf
- Leafy vegetables
- Dark chocolate
- Coffee
- Grapefruit

# Garlicky Oniony Flaky Pancake

**Hot water pastry works by hindering gluten formation and cooking the proteins; this means this type of dough is a lot less stretchy and will break more easily, which is perfect for creating a flaky dough. When the dough is layered, like we're doing to make this pancake, it'll create beautiful flaky layers.**

SERVES 4

**Essential Equipment**
Large non-stick frying pan or cast-iron pan; small blender; rolling pin

350g/12½oz plain flour, plus extra for shaping
50ml/1½fl oz toasted sesame oil
4 spring onions, roughly chopped
½ tsp salt
6 garlic cloves, peeled

HOW TO ROLL FLAKY PANCAKES

**1.** Put the flour in a large bowl and add 200ml/7fl oz boiling water. Stir with a wooden spoon until it forms a dough.

**2.** Tip the dough out on a surface and knead until smooth, then place in a clean bowl, cover and leave to rest for 30 minutes.

**3.** Blend half the sesame oil with the spring onions, salt and garlic to make a fine paste.

**4.** Cut the dough into 4 pieces. Take one and keep the rest covered in the bowl.

**5.** Lightly flour the dough and roll it into a ball, then roll the dough out to a 20cm/8in-diameter circle. Spread 1–2 tablespoons of the herby oil over the top like topping a pizza, then take one edge and roll into a long sausage. Next, roll the sausage into a spiral, tucking the tail underneath.

**6.** Gently press the spiral to flatten, flour the dough, then roll out again to a 17.5cm/7in circle.

**7.** Repeat with the remaining dough pieces.

**8.** Heat the rest of the oil in a large frying pan over a medium-high heat. Once hot, cook the pancakes for 2 minutes on each side until golden and crisp.

**9.** Remove and drain on kitchen paper.

**10.** These pancakes go great with any sauce but I love Funky Chilli Sauce (p. 249) and Japanese Mayo (p. 251).

**Tip**
You could also top them with mozzarella and make them cheesy. Whack them in the oven for herby cheesy flaky garlicky bread. See you later, garlic baguette.

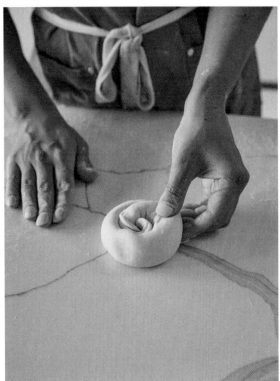

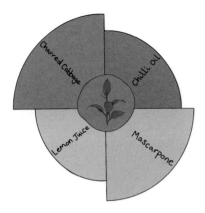

# Smoky Hispi Cabbage with Chilli Oil (V)

I feel like cabbage is so underrated. It's one of the most cost-effective vegetables that, when treated right, becomes a highlight of many restaurant-goers' meals. Let me share with you how restaurants make cabbage the most delicious dish you eat. Smoke. Chilli. Fat.

SERVES 4 AS A SIDE

**Essential Equipment**
Large frying pan or cast-iron pan

1 hispi cabbage or sweetheart
    cabbage
2 tbsp olive oil
Large pinch of salt
2 tbsp butter or plant-based
    butter
½ tbsp lemon juice
6 tbsp mascarpone, softened
2 tbsp Philli's Chilli Oil (p. 250)
    or 1 tbsp shop-bought chilli oil
½ bunch chives, chopped
2 tbsp Crispy Things (p. 252) or
    crispy shallots

**1.** Peel away the outer leaves and quarter the cabbage.

**2.** Heat a large frying pan (preferably cast iron) with olive oil and sprinkle salt over the cut side of the cabbage.

**3.** Sear the cabbage on the cut sides until all the surface is charred.

**4.** Flip so the cut side is face up and add enough water to just cover half of the cabbage, as well as the butter.

**5.** Allow to poach until all the water is evaporated, turning the cabbage gently with tongs every 5 minutes. The cabbage should be completely tender. When the water has nearly evaporated, turn off the heat and coat the cabbage in the melted butter from the pan using a spoon. Finish with the lemon juice.

**6.** Whisk the mascarpone with a fork and smear it onto a plate using the back of a spoon. Add the cabbage and drizzle with the remaining butter and chilli oil, then top with chopped chives and Crispy Things.

**Taste** everything all together **and adjust**; if you want more spice, add chilli oil or if it's too hot add more mascarpone.

# Fennel and Cucumber Slaw ⓥ

Fennel and cucumber are the perfect partner for a little fishy dish, and this slaw is super punchy with Dijon mustard. You can use this dressing as your classic salad dressing: whip it up and you're done.

SERVES 4 AS A SIDE

**Essential Equipment**
Mandoline or super sharp knife

1 fennel
1 cucumber
½ tbsp salt
1 tbsp Philli's Chilli Oil (p. 250)
   or shop-bought chilli oil
2 tbsp rice vinegar
2 tbsp sesame oil
2 tsp Dijon mustard
2 tsp honey or sugar
½ tsp sesame seeds

TO SERVE
Miso and Gochu Marinated Cod
   (p. 234) or Spicy Green Fish
   Cakes (p. 204)

**1.** Chop off the top of the fennel and reserve the fronds (because they look pretty for garnishing).

**2.** Slice the fennel and cucumber with a mandoline or knife to 2mm thick (be super careful and always use the guard or a super sharp knife).

**3.** Mix together the salt, chilli oil, rice vinegar, sesame oil, Dijon mustard and honey.

**4.** Toss the veg with the dressing. Top with sesame seeds and fennel fronds.

**Taste and adjust** just before serving.

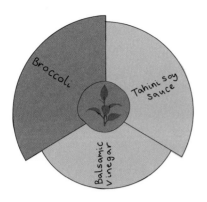

# Charred Broccoli, Balsamic Red Onions and Tahini Soy Sauce ⓥᵉ

This is hands down the best broccoli dish. It's beaut. If you're not into broc, this side dish is about to change your opinion. Charred broc, rich tahini and sweet sticky red onions.

SERVES 4 AS A SIDE

**Essential Equipment**
Large frying pan or cast-iron pan with lid

3 small red onions, unpeeled
1 tbsp oil
3 tbsp balsamic vinegar
6 tbsp water
2 tbsp sesame oil
250–350g/9–12½oz tenderstem broc, trimmed and big spears sliced in half
Pinch of salt
Tahini Soy Sauce (p. 251)
Sprinkle of sesame seeds

**1.** Preheat the oven to 180°C (160°C fan oven) Gas 4.

**2.** Slice the onions in half down the cross section, leaving the skin on.

**3.** Put the oil, balsamic vinegar and water in a small foil-lined oven tray and place the onions, cut side down, onto the tray.

**4.** Roast for 45–50 minutes until a deep caramel colour but make sure the oven tray doesn't burn. Remove and allow to rest.

**5** While the onions are roasting, make the Tahini Soy Sauce (p. 245).

**6.** Heat the sesame oil in a frying pan with a lid over a high heat, add the broccoli spears and sprinkle with salt. Cook for 5 minutes, until caramelised. Add 50ml/1½fl oz water, put on the lid and shake for a further 2 minutes. This will steam the broc. Remove from the heat.

**7.** Carefully remove the skins from the onions, making sure you leave the halved onions intact by cutting the skins off at the top.

**8.** Smear the Tahini Soy Sauce on a plate.

**9.** Top with the broccoli and red onions and sprinkle with sesame seeds.

This is a simple dish, but you can play with the balance as you **taste and adjust.**

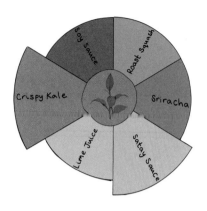

# Crispy Kale and Squash
# with Satay Sauce

**Peanuts, greens and squash make the perfect friends. Peanut satay sauce is excellent: smeared under sweet roasted squash and bitter salted greens it makes the perfect side dish.**

SERVES 4 AS A SIDE

100g/3½oz kale
½ butternut squash (round end),
　skin left on
2 tbsp olive oil
Pinch of flaky sea salt
½ tsp sesame seeds
No-Cook Satay Sauce (p. 252)

**1.** Preheat the oven to 220°C (200°C fan oven) Gas 7.

**2.** Rinse and drain the kale, then remove and discard the centre stalks and slice the leaves.

**3.** Cut the half butternut in half again to expose the middle. Remove the seeds with a spoon and slice into 1cm/½in wedges.

**4.** Place the butternut onto an oven tray, drizzle with the olive oil and sprinkle with salt. Roast for 30–35 minutes.

**5.** Make the No-cook Satay Sauce (p. 252).

**6.** After 30 minutes add the kale and mix together on the tray, then sprinkle the sesame seeds over and roast for a further 7–10 minutes. Watch the kale as it can burn easily. Make sure the veg is caramelised and crisp.

**7.** Remove from the oven. Smear satay sauce on the plate, then top with the sesame roasted veg.

This is a simple dish, but you can play with the balance as you **taste and adjust.**

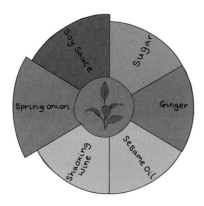

# Cantonese-Style Steamed Fish

Cantonese steamed fish is a celebration dish that is served at banquets and comes out during a long tasting menu. At weddings, a similar version is made with a whole fish. Now I also love 'en papillote', when the fish, meat or veggies is encased in a parchment parcel. The beauty of this method is that you can prep it before and then everyone gets to open their own little present and they get a face full of steamed fish. It's just a few ingredients and makes a great weeknight meal.

SERVES 4

**Essential Equipment**
Baking parchment

2 tbsp Shaoxing wine
2 tbsp soy sauce
1 tsp sugar
1 tsp sesame oil
4 spring onions, julienned
5cm/2in piece of ginger,
   thinly sliced
4 sea bass fillets

TO SERVE
Fennel and Cucumber Slaw
   (p. 196) or Gunpowder Pots
   (p. 168)

STEAM FISH IN PARCHMENT

**1.** Preheat the oven to 200°C (180°C fan oven) Gas 6.

**2.** Mix the Shaoxing, soy sauce, sugar and sesame oil.

**3.** Cut four 30cm/12in squares of baking parchment.

**4.** Add half the spring onions and ginger to one half of each paper square, distribute the sauce on the pieces of paper then add the fish, skin side up. Then add the rest of the spring onion and ginger on top of the fish skin.

**5.** Bring the sides over and fold in half, then seal the edges and place on an oven tray.

**6.** Cook in the oven for 10–15 minutes, until it reaches an internal temperature of 45–50°C.

**7.** Remove from the oven and serve immediately. Allow everyone to open their own steamed fish present.

**Taste and adjust** to your palate.

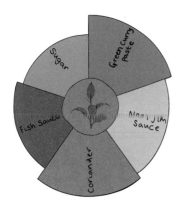

# Spicy Green Fish Cakes

These fish cakes are inspired by the bouncy Thai fish cakes that I just love to dip. Going against tradition, I'm using Thai green curry paste as the main flavouring to add a pack of herby punch. Super fresh and light, and if you're serving these as appetisers or snacks, they go perfectly with the Tofu Nuggz (p. 170) and a cheeky Green Nam Jim (p. 254), Funky Chilli Sauce (p. 249) and Japanese Mayo (p. 251).

SERVES 4/MAKES 20–24 CAKES

**Essential Equipment**
Blender

500g/1lb 1½oz white fish fillets, skinless and pin boned
2 tbsp green curry paste (p. 207) or shop-bought
1 tbsp fish sauce or ½ tbsp soy sauce
1 tsp sugar
2 egg whites
40g/1½oz rice flour or cornflour
Large handful of coriander leaves, finely chopped
4 spring onions, finely sliced
10 green beans, finely sliced
½ tsp chilli flakes
Oil for shallow frying

TO SERVE
Green Nam Jim (p. 254)
1:2 ratio Funky Chilli Sauce (p. 249) and Japanese Mayo (p. 251)

**1.** Make the green curry paste (p. 207) prior to beginning the recipe.

**2.** Slice the fish into chunks and put in a blender with the green curry paste, fish sauce, sugar and egg whites. Blend to a fine paste.

**3.** Use a spatula to remove the paste into a bowl, and mix in the rice flour followed by the coriander, spring onions, green beans and chilli flakes.

**4.** Heat a wok or frying pan with a thin layer of oil to 160°C.

**5.** Lightly oil your hands to stop the fish mix sticking. Take a heaped tablespoonful and shape into a mini burger patty, then slide the fish cake into the oil, cooking just one fish cake to start with.

**6.** Fry for 2 minutes before flipping and frying until golden on all sides and piping hot in the middle.

**7.** Remove and drain on kitchen paper.

**8. Taste the fish cake and adjust the mix** to your palate before frying the rest of the fish cakes, approximately six at a time. You might like a little extra fish sauce or herbs.

**9.** Serve the fish cakes with Nam Jim, Funky Chilli Sauce and Japanese Mayo.

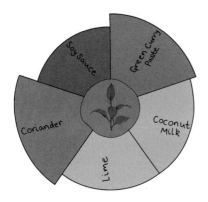

# Green Curry Mussels

I was in my late teens when I had a real Thai green curry for the first time. It became a bit of an obsession. Each town I visited, I had to have one. From Ko Pha-Ngan to KFC in Bangkok they were exactly what was required in the Thai summer heat, and I had a few. I'm making a green curry paste for this recipe; in Thailand coriander root is often used, however it's quite hard to find outside of Thailand so I'm subbing with stems. If you want to buy your curry paste, that's totally legit as well. Can you just make a promise to me and please de-beard your mussels? It sends shivers down my body thinking about beardy mussels. Hold the mussel in your hand and with the other pull any stringy bit with one firm pull out of the shell.

SERVES 4 AS A STARTER OR
2–3 AS A MAIN

## Essential Equipment
Large heavy pot with lid; small blender

FOR THE GREEN CURRY PASTE
30 green bird's eye chillies or
    rocket chillies, sliced
10 limes leaves or zest of
    3 lime, finely grated
1 tbsp coriander stems,
    finely sliced
2 Thai shallots, sliced or
    1 banana shallot, sliced
2 garlic cloves
2.5cm/1in piece of ginger, minced
1.5cm/½in galangal or
    1 tsp galangal paste or
    horseradish paste
1 tsp shrimp paste or 1 tsp miso
½ tsp ground coriander

50g/1½oz salt
1kg/2lb 3oz fresh mussels
½ tbsp oil
400ml/14fl oz full-fat coconut
    milk, unshaken
2 lemongrass sticks, sliced
2 tbsp green curry paste
    (homemade or shop-bought)
4 garlic cloves, sliced

2 tsp soy sauce
Handful of chopped coriander
2 green chillies, sliced
1 lime, wedged

————

**1.** Blend all the green curry paste ingredients with just enough water to make a smooth paste. If you have a large pestle and mortar and patience, you can also use this method. Store the paste in an airtight container in the fridge for up to 2 weeks.

**2.** Mix the salt with 1 litre of water in a large bowl, then add the mussels and allow them to sit for 15 minutes. This makes the mussels think they're still in the sea and removes any sand.

**3.** Remove the beard: hold the mussel and pull out the stringy bit firmly and throw out, then place the mussel in a new bowl of fresh water. Discard any mussels that are broken or stay open when tapped.

**4.** Put the oil and the solid white coconut fat from the top of the can into a large lidded saucepan. Heat until it splits then fry the lemongrass, green curry paste and garlic for 2 minutes.

**5.** Add the cleaned, drained mussels, the rest of the coconut milk and soy sauce, turn up the heat and close the lid. Cook for 3–4 minutes and shake the pan.

**6.** Remove the lid and the mussels should be open. (Discard any that remain closed.)

**7.** Turn off the heat and add chopped coriander and chillies. **Taste and adjust** to your palate. Serve with lime wedges.

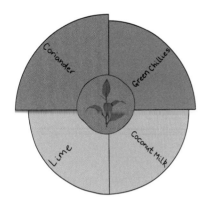

# Coriander and Coconut Chicken Curry

Bright green and coconutty, it doesn't get much better than this. This curry is based on the fish curry I made in the *MasterChef* kitchen. The trick to keeping it bright green is not to cook the coriander. The more you cook it the darker it gets, so throw in your coconut coriander mix right at the very end just before serving.

SERVES 4

**Essential Equipment**
Stick blender; large heavy frying pan

1 tbsp neutral oil
8 skin-on chicken thighs, bone in
5–10 green chillies, finely
    chopped
Pinch of salt
400ml/14fl oz coconut milk
1 large bunch of coriander leaves
    plus a handful of chopped for
    garnishing
1 medium onion, sliced
5cm/2in piece of ginger, minced
4 garlic cloves, minced
½ tbsp ground cumin
1 tbsp ground coriander
Juice of 1 lime

TO SERVE
BBBR (p. 130)

**1.** Heat the oil in a large heavy frying pan over a medium heat. Add the chicken thighs, skin side down, with a pinch of salt and caramelise for 5–10 minutes until golden. Do not touch for the first few minutes so you don't tear the skin. Depending on the size of your pan you may need to work in batches.

**2.** Meanwhile take a green chilli and taste a little bit to find out how hot your chillies are. Then blend 5–10 green chillies, the thick, white half of the coconut milk and the coriander leaves to a smooth paste.

**3.** Remove the thighs and set aside. Add the onion to the frying pan with a pinch of salt and fry until golden – about 5 minutes. The chicken should have released its fat to cook the onions; however, if it looks a little dry add a tablespoon of neutral oil. Follow with the ginger and garlic and fry for another 2 minutes.

**4.** Add the ground cumin and coriander with the rest of the coconut milk and then add in the chicken thighs, being careful not to wet the chicken skin.

**5.** Poach the chicken uncovered over a medium heat for 25–30 minutes until super soft and the internal temperature is over 70°C.

**6.** Add the coriander, coconut milk and chilli mix around the chicken, being careful not to wet the crispy chicken skin, and allow to come to the boil.

**7.** Finish with lime juice and more chopped coriander.

**Taste and adjust** to your palate.

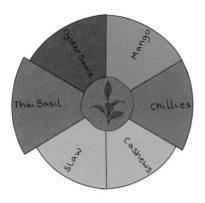

# Mango and Thai Basil Pulled Chicken Flatbreads

**Okay, we have wraps fairly regularly and this one is a weeknight fave as it's super quick and packed with flavour.**

SERVES 4

**Essential Equipment**
Sharp knife or mandoline; oven tray

1 garlic clove, minced
2.5cm/1in piece of ginger, minced
4 Thai chillies or red chillies, sliced
4 tbsp oyster sauce
2 tbsp soy sauce
2 tsp honey
2 tsp olive oil
100g/3½oz cashews
4 chicken breasts
1 mango, diced
Large handful of Thai basil, or standard basil, leaves only

FOR THE RED CABBAGE SLAW
¼ small red cabbage, finely shredded using mandoline or super sharp knife
4 tbsp rice vinegar
2 tbsp honey
A pinch of salt

TO SERVE
12 My Mum's Chapatis (p. 116) or 8 large flatbreads or 8 wraps
Drizzle of Japanese Mayo (p. 251) or Kewpie mayo
Drizzle of Funky Chilli Sauce (p. 249) or sriracha

**1.** Preheat the oven to 180°C (160°C fan oven) Gas 4.

**2.** Mix together the garlic, ginger, Thai chillies, oyster sauce, soy sauce, honey, olive oil and cashews. Marinate the chicken breasts, preferably overnight but for at least 2 hours.

**3.** Put the chicken with the marinade in an oven tray and roast for 25–30 minutes until its internal temperature reaches 65°C.

**4.** Slice the red cabbage and mix with the rice vinegar, honey and salt. Leave to marinate for 20–30 minutes.

**5.** Once cooked, remove the chicken from the oven, allow to rest for 5 minutes and pull with a fork. Mix the marinade back through, add the mango and basil to the chicken and allow to warm in the oven for a further 5 minutes.

**6.** Serve with warmed chapatis and the cabbage slaw. Build the wraps and drizzle in Japanese Mayo (p. 251) and Funky Chilli Sauce (p. 249), then finish with more sliced chilli.

**Taste and adjust** all the flavours together as you eat.

**Tip**
To warm many chapatis or flatbreads at the same time, splash with water and seal in a foil parcel then heat in the oven for 5 minutes at 180°C (160°C fan oven) Gas 4.

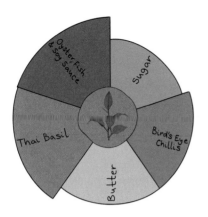

# *Fancy* Thai Basil Beef Steaks

**The main differences between a restaurant steak and a home-cooked steak are the quality of meat and the cut. So if you can, pop to your local butcher and ask for a thick-cut steak. To get that deep caramel crust on the outside you need to cook it longer than you think, and if the steak is too thin, it'll overcook. Get a chunky piece, cook it in a heavy pan (preferably cast iron) when it's smoking, and get a deep colour on that beef, with only oil to start with. Then add butter, baste and when the beef hits an internal temperature of 45–50°C take it out and rest it to 54–57°C. Then slice it against the grain and share between two people. Perfect every time.**

SERVES 4

**Essential Equipment**
Large heavy ovenproof frying pan, preferably cast iron, or preheated oven tray

2 x 400g/14oz beef sirloin or
    bavette steaks
2 tbsp oil
Liberal sprinkle of salt and fresh
    cracked black pepper
50g/1½oz cold butter, diced
2 red peppers, thinly sliced
1 white onion, thinly sliced
5 garlic cloves, sliced
2 red bird's eye chillies, sliced
2 tbsp soy sauce
1 tbsp oyster sauce
1 tbsp fish sauce
2 tsp sugar
Large handful of Thai basil
    leaves
Sprinkle of flaky sea salt

SIZZLE THAT STEAK

**1.** Get the steak out of the fridge 20 minutes before cooking, remove the packaging, wrap in kitchen paper and pat fully dry, otherwise you won't get a good crust.

**2.** Turn on the extractor fan: it's about to get smoky.

**3.** Heat a large heavy frying pan over a high heat. Rub each steak with oil and then liberally add salt and pepper.

**4.** Working one at a time, sear the steaks on both sides for 2–3 minutes until it has a nice char then transfer to an oven tray. Probe the steak: you should be looking for an internal temperature of 45–50°C. Keep the frying pan warm but wipe clean any charred bits with kitchen paper. Repeat with the second steak.

**5.** Using tongs, hold both steaks fat-side down in the pan for 2–3 minutes until the fat is golden. Then allow to lie flat and add the butter, spooning it over the steaks as it foams.

**6.** Remove the steaks and place back on the oven tray. Pour over half the butter and allow to rest for 10 minutes.

**7.** Place the same pan over a high heat and add the red pepper and onions. Cook for 5 minutes. Add the garlic and chillies and turn down the heat. Cook for a further minute before adding the soy, oyster and fish sauces and sugar.

**8.** Allow the sauce to thicken, then remove from the heat and tear in the Thai basil leaves.

**9.** Plate the vegetables and then slice the steak in 2cm slices using a super sharp knife against the grain. Serve with a sprinkle of flaky salt.

**Taste** all the flavours together and make any notes to amend for next time.

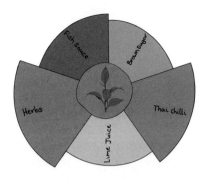

# Pork Larb

Laarb, laap or larp is the national dish of Laos. It's a salad made up mainly of meat. What more could you want? You can switch it up with different meats – make it with chicken, beef or mushrooms, and obvs add loads of herbs. In Laos it usually contains a powder made from toasted rice grains, which gives a beautiful nutty flavour and texture.

SERVES 4

**Essential Equipment**
Wok or large frying pan; pestle and mortar

1 tbsp any white rice (optional)
1 tbsp oil
500g/1lb 1½oz pork mince
½ tbsp chilli powder
1 tsp brown sugar
1 tbsp fish sauce
4 Thai chillies, sliced, or
    2 chillies, sliced, for milder
    heat
Juice of 1 lime
4 Thai shallots or 1 banana
    shallot or ½ small red onion,
    sliced
Handful of Thai basil or normal
    basil, roughly chopped
Handful of mint, roughly
    chopped
Handful of coriander, roughly
    chopped
4 spring onions, sliced

TO SERVE
Crispy Things (p. 252)
Sticky rice

**1.** Everything comes together quite quickly so make sure you do the chopping beforehand.

**2.** Toast the rice in a dry wok or frying pan until it smells like popcorn and looks golden. Transfer to a pestle and mortar or whizzer and blend into a powder.

**3.** Heat a wok or frying pan over a high heat and add the oil, then add the pork and fry until there are no pink bits left.

**4.** Add the toasted rice powder, chilli powder, brown sugar, fish sauce, Thai chillies and lime juice and fry for another minute.

**5.** Add the shallots, herbs and spring onions and fry for a final minute before **tasting and adjusting** to your palate.

# 1-Ingredient Dark Chocolate Pots and Raspberry Jam

Hervé This is one of my heroes. He is a physical chemist who came up with the idea to change the structure of chocolate by adding water to it, emulsifying and then whipping and cooling to add air and structure into the chocolate, when it chills and forms a deep, intensely rich chocolate pot. This was super interesting for me as, if you've ever worked with chocolate, you'll know that adding just a drop of water to chocolate can change the stability of its structure and cause it to harden like a rock. The beauty of this dessert it doesn't mask the flavour of the chocolate so make sure to use a chocolate you love!

SERVES 4–6

**Essential Equipment**
Hand whisk; 2 bowls (preferably metal)

Plenty of ice cubes
225g/8oz chocolate (70% cocoa solids – choose a high-quality chocolate you love)
4 tbsp raspberry jam

**1.** Have a large bowl of ice prepared.

**2.** Mix the chocolate with 170ml/6fl oz water in a small saucepan and heat over a low heat until fully emulsified and melted.

**3.** Pour the chocolate mixture into another bowl and set it over the ice bowl and start to whisk into a chilled foam.

**4.** Just as it starts to look glossy and with the consistency of lightly whipped double cream, quickly take the bowl off the ice.

**5.** Spoon your favourite jam into the bottom of the pot and then top with the chocolate mousse. It should be set at room temperature; however, if it looks a little runny pop it in the fridge for 10 minutes.

**Note**
If you leave the mixture on the ice too long it will set too hard to spoon; you simply need to re-melt it and whip again.

# DARK
# HORSE

Chefs and cooks today are obsessed with umami, which is a Japanese word meaning yumminess or savouriness. Umami ingredients are used to add depth to a dish. Umami flavouring comes from glutamate, an amino acid derivative, paired with sodium. As soon as the monosodium glutamate (MSG) dissolves in your saliva, it is broken down into glutamate and sodium (Na+) to give the savoury, salty flavour we associate with umami.

Glutamic acid is acidified glutamate. It is the most present naturally occurring amino acid found in proteins. When we taste glutamates we naturally associate them with proteins, because when protein is digested in our bodies, glutamic acid and other free amino acids are released. We need glutamic acid for protein synthesis and to act as a neurotransmitter. Regardless of the source of glutamate – whether it's an aged steak, ripe tomatoes or refined MSG – our bodies use it in the same way.

Glutamates are naturally found in many ingredients like sundried tomatoes, dried mushrooms, miso, soy sauce and Parmesan cheese. There are little salty crystals in aged Parmesan, which is naturally produced MSG. Next time you're eating an aged cheese, notice the little crystals of MSG salt on your tongue.

## CHEFS AND COOKS TODAY ARE OBSESSED WITH UMAMI, WHICH IS A JAPANESE WORD MEANING YUMMINESS OR SAVOURINESS. UMAMI INGREDIENTS ARE USED TO ADD DEPTH TO A DISH.

Dashi, an umami-rich stock, is the heart of Japanese cuisine. At its base is kombu (dried kelp) and dried bonito flakes. In 1908, Kikunae Ikeda, a Japanese chemist, discovered the flavour chemical that makes dashi so delicious. It was MSG, or E621 (the European E number). Ikeda went on to isolate this compound and refine it, eventually launching Aji No Moto, a company specialising in the production of MSG. The love of MSG soon spread through Eastern Asia and the USA.

However, in 1968 Robert Ho Man Kwok M.D. wrote an anecdotal paper on the effects of MSG, including numbness of the neck, arms and back, headache, dizziness and palpitations that he experienced following the consumption of Chinese food. He linked this effect with MSG, later dubbed 'Chinese restaurant syndrome'. This letter was later picked up to be a hoax and many studies have been carried out that disprove Kwok's theory; however, the myth still remains ingrained in Western belief. It took until 2020 for the American Merriam-Webster dictionary to update the definition of *Chinese restaurant syndrome*. It notes, 'Chinese restaurant syndrome has been criticized as misleading and potentially offensive.' In the 1990s the American FDA recognised that MSG was perfectly safe for consumption of about 2g for someone weighing 70kg/11 stone. If you were to overconsume MSG like you were to overconsume salt or sugar you might feel a little ill, but just be sensible. If MSG was so dangerous then why does Japan, where the product was first discovered, have one of the world's highest life expectancies?

Today chefs and scientists are trying to educate home cooks that MSG is not so scary, and, when consumed at levels similar to our consumption of salt, it's perfectly safe and, more importantly, delicious. I hope now you will try to add a little more umami to your cooking whether it be a few sundried tomatoes, a tablespoon of miso or grab a bag of MSG.

I find it hard to distinguish between salt and umami as so often these ingredients are paired together. For example, soy sauce and miso are umami, however both are also very salty. The recipes in this chapter showcase the depth found in the use of umami ingredients that we all crave.

## Dark Horse ingredients

- Miso
- Mushrooms
- Soy sauce
- MSG
- Katsuobushi
- Nutritional yeast
- Shitake mushrooms
- Fish sauce
- Black garlic

# Chicken Yakitori with Togarashi Spice

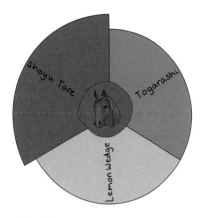

SERVES 4

**Essential Equipment**
8 soaked bamboo skewers

FOR THE YAKITORI
6 chicken thighs, skin on
6 spring onions
Sprinkle of sea salt
100ml/3½fl oz sake
   (preferably in a spray bottle)

Shoyu Tare (p. 255)
Sprinkle of togarashi
1 lemon, wedged

PREPARING CHICKEN SKEWERS

I love negima yakitori. It's found in many izakaya restaurants, which are like Japanese pubs. These skewers are comprised of fatty chicken thighs and crunchy fresh spring onions which are barbecued with a tare.

I love cooking my skewers on a charcoal barbecue. You get the most flavour using a fan to blow smoke onto the chicken. I like to use binchotan, a traditional Japanese charcoal, which is formed from a single piece of wood and can burn up to 1000°C/2400°F for 3–5 hours. You want to cook the skewers when the coals are white. Sake is sprayed on the chicken beforehand to create an even cook. Keep your kitchen scissors handy as if you have any burning bits you can just snip them off. These skewers are best served on a warm day with a cold beer.

**1.** Prepare the chicken. If the thighs have a bone in the middle, remove the bone and then cut the thigh into 2 equal pieces against the grain.

**2.** Cut the light green and white parts of the spring onions into 3cm/1¼in pieces.

**3.** With the skewer pointing away from you, pierce the chicken skin of the left side a chicken thigh half and roll the meat so the skin is face outwards, concave and plump, then pierce a piece of spring onion tightly against the chicken on the left side. Then repeat with another piece of thigh meat followed by another spring onion, then another piece of thigh meat.

**4.** Pierce the right side of the chicken with a second skewer feeding through the meat and spring onion so that you have 2 skewers going through 3 thigh halves and 2 pieces of spring onion.

**5.** Slice in-between the skewers so you end up with 2 skewers: chicken, spring onion, chicken, spring onion, chicken.

**6.** Press the meat together with your hand and make sure the skewer is crowded, as leaving too much room can dry the meat out.

**7.** Trim the sides of the skewers so they are even.

**8.** Make the Shoyu Tare, then transfer to a high-sided container to be brushed onto the meat later.

**9.** If using a griddle pan, sprinkle salt on the skewers with a shaker or using a three-finger pinch from a distance, making sure to coat all the skewers.

**10.** Spray or brush the sake over the chicken skewers.

**11.** Heat the pan over a medium heat and fry the skewers on each side until golden and cooked through: 5–7 minutes in batches. Then brush all the skewers with the Shoyu Tare and glaze for 30 seconds. Keep an eye as the sugar can caramelise easily in the pan.

**12.** Remove, sprinkle over a dusting of togorashi spice and serve with a wedge of lemon.

**Taste and adjust** by adding more lemon or togorashi if you like.

**Tip**
The skewers are best on the barbecue. Light the barbecue and make sure the coal flames have burnt out and they're completely white. This will take 45–60 minutes.

Pop the skewers on the barbecue and flip the chicken every minute – you don't want anything to catch at this point – and keep that meat super juicy.

After about 5–7 minutes you'll see the chicken turn golden. Dip or brush the Shoyu Tare over the chicken and put the skewers back on the barbecue. The chicken will caramelise quite quickly now. Cook for a further 30 seconds. Then serve with togarashi and lemon.

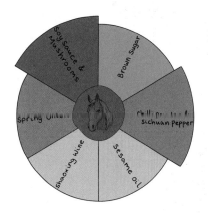

# Soy-Glazed King Oyster Mushroom 'Murger' Pitas Ⓥᵉ

If you haven't experienced Muslim Chinese food before I encourage you to head to your local restaurant or get yourself to North Western China to taste it for yourself. I first had Muslim Chinese food in Xi'an where the streets are filled with bustling vendors and delicious smells.

There's a dish called a rou jia mo or Chinese 'murger' which is chopped-up juicy meat in a fluffy pita and almost looks like a hamburger. This is the kind of street food I got on board with. I am using king oyster mushrooms for their meaty texture and hitting them with a ton of spices to make these sandwiches super yum.

If you don't have the time to make your own pitas, simply pick up a pack from the shops and skip to step 4.

SERVES 4, 2 PITAS EACH

**Essential Equipment**
Heavy frying pan with lid; rolling pin; serrated knife

FOR THE PITAS
300g/10½oz plain flour
1½ tsp active dry yeast
½ tsp salt

FOR THE PULLED MUSHROOMS
600g/1lb 5oz king oyster
    mushrooms
4 tbsp sesame oil
1 tsp Sichuan peppercorns,
    hand ground (optional)
1 tsp cumin seeds
1 tsp chilli powder
3 tbsp Shaoxing wine
2 tbsp soy sauce
2.5cm/1in piece of ginger
½ tsp ground cinnamon
4 spring onions, finely sliced
2 tbsp brown sugar

TO SERVE
Funky Chilli Sauce (p. 249) or
    sriracha
Japanese Mayo (p. 251) or
    Kewpie mayo

**1.** Mix the flour, yeast and salt together, then slowly add 160ml/6fl oz warm water until a smooth dough forms. You might need to adjust with a touch more flour or water depending on your flour.

**2.** Knead the dough for 10 minutes by hand (or in a stand mixer) to work the gluten. Form into a ball, place in a clean bowl and cover.

**3.** Leave to prove until it's doubled in size, about an hour.

**4.** While the dough is proving, shred the raw mushrooms using a fork. Heat a large frying pan over a high heat with sesame oil and add the pulled mushrooms. Cook for 5 minutes, turning the mushrooms with tongs, before adding the Sichuan peppercorns, cumin seeds and chilli powder and cooking for a further 2 minutes.

**5.** Add the Shaoxing wine and cook down for 3 minutes until the alcohol has evaporated, then turn down the heat and add the soy sauce, ginger, cinnamon and 100ml/3½fl oz water. Allow the mushrooms to fry until all the liquid has evaporated.

**6.** Finish with spring onions and brown sugar. **Taste and adjust**.

**7.** Punch out the dough to remove all the air bubbles and divide into 8 equal pieces. Cover the dough and work with one piece at a time.

**8.** Roll a piece of dough into a long sausage shape, spiral the dough around the centre and tuck the edge in. Press the dough out with your palm and then roll it out to 8–10cm/3½–4in in diameter. Dust with flour and then cover with a dry cloth and leave to prove for 20 minutes while you roll out the rest of the dough.

**9.** Heat a splash of sesame oil in a heavy frying pan (preferably cast iron) with a lid. Working 2 pieces at a time, carefully lift the dough (I like to use a dough scraper) and place in the pan. Cook over a medium heat with the lid on for 2 minutes. Remove the lid, flip and cook for a further 2 minutes.

**10.** Repeat with the remaining dough pieces.

**11.** Reheat the mushrooms and cut the pitas with a bread knife. Fill the pitas with the pulled mushroom mix and serve with hot sauce and Japanese Mayo (p. 251).

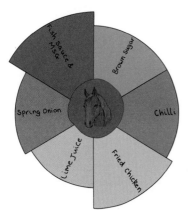

# Fish Sauce Chicken Wings

One of my favourite places to eat wings in London is Smoking Goat, which I believe was inspired by Pok Pok NY. I never had the chance to eat at Pok Pok, but MY GOD these wings are to die for. You might think fish sauce and chicken wings are a weird combo, but please go with me. Make these wings next time there's a sports match or the sun is out.

SERVES 4

**Essential Equipment**
Wok; tongs

FOR THE WINGS
1kg/2lb 3oz /12 chicken wings
1 tbsp fish sauce
1 tsp garlic powder
1 chicken stock cube, crumbled, or 1 tsp chicken gravy granules, ground
½ tsp ground white pepper
1 tsp MSG (optional)
1 tsp baking powder
40g/1½oz cornflour
90g/3oz plain flour
400–500ml/14–18fl oz neutral oil for frying

FOR THE STICKY FISH SAUCE
3 tbsp fish sauce
4 tbsp brown sugar
2 small red chillies, finely sliced
Juice of 1 lime

1 tbsp roasted peanuts, ground into a powder
2 spring onions, finely sliced
1 tsp sesame seeds

**1.** Cut the wings into tips and drumettes.

**2.** Marinate the wings in the fish sauce, garlic powder, chicken stock, white pepper and MSG (if using) for a minimum of 2 hours but preferably overnight.

**3.** To make the sauce, heat the fish sauce and brown sugar together to dissolve, remove from the heat and stir in the chillies and lime juice.

**4.** Mix the baking powder, cornflour and plain flour together.

**5.** Preheat the oven to 180°C (160°C fan oven) Gas 4. Turn on the extractor fan and fill a large pan or wok with oil, making sure not to overfill but deep enough to deep-fry the wings. Heat the oil to 170°C.

**6.** Remove the wings from the marinade, coat each piece in the cornflour mixture and really scrunch the starch into the wing.

**7.** Deep fry for 5–7 minutes, working in batches and making sure not to overcrowd the pan.

**8.** Using tongs, remove the pieces and drain on a prepared tray with kitchen paper. Repeat with the other pieces.

**9.** Place the wings on an oven tray and roast in the oven for 12–15 minutes until fully cooked through and crispy.

**10.** Drench the wings in the sauce, then top with peanuts, spring onions and sesame seeds.

**Taste** and make any amends as you eat.

**Note**
Serve with hand wipes and bibs.

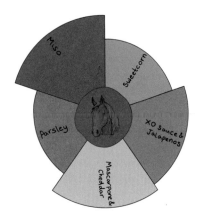

# Cheesy Miso XO Corn

**This is really tasty and levels up your sad steamed sweetcorn on a Tuesday night. A super side dish in under 10 minutes.**

SERVES 4 AS A SIDE

**Essential Equipment**
Saucepan

500g/1lb 1½oz frozen sweetcorn
2 tbsp olive oil
100g/3½oz mascarpone or
    plant-based spread
50g/1½oz Cheddar cheese or
    plant-based cheese
1 tsp chilli flakes
1 tbsp miso
200ml/7fl oz milk or oat milk
Handful of parsley, chopped
2 fresh jalapenos, finely sliced,
    or any sliced chilli
1 tbsp Cheat XO Sauce (p. 255) or
    1 tbsp Philli's Chilli Oil (p. 250)
    (optional)

**1.** Defrost the sweetcorn in water and then strain it through a colander.

**2.** Heat a heavy-based frying pan with olive oil over a high heat until it's smoking.

**3.** Add the sweetcorn away from you and char on all sides for 5 minutes – it should smell like popcorn.

**4.** Mix together the mascarpone, Cheddar cheese, chilli flakes, miso and milk. Turn down the heat to low, add the mix into the frying pan and allow it to melt together and thicken.

**5. Taste and adjust** to your palate.

**6.** Turn off the heat, add the parsley, top with jalapenos and drizzle over some XO sauce or chilli oil.

# Shitake Okonomiyaki

Okonomiyaki is a special dish for me as it's the first dish I did on *MasterChef*. It's the street food that made me love Osaka and it's the food I would eat late at night in Hong Kong after a long shift in the restaurant. It's Japanese soul food at its finest. Okonomi means 'how you like it', and yaki means 'to grill', so I'm linking it with beaut umami mushrooms. If you can get your hands on porcini powder, it makes all the difference. You can play around with flavours; I also love prawns, kimchi and cheese. Get creative and have fun.

SERVES 2

**Essential Equipment**
Mandoline or super sharp knife; large non-stick frying pan or large frying pan and baking parchment; oven gloves; large pizza tray

240g/8½oz/about ½ small white
  cabbage, finely shredded
2 spring onions, finely sliced
20g/½oz sushi ginger, chopped
  (optional)
80g/3oz plain flour
½ tsp salt
1 tsp sugar
1 tsp baking powder
1 tsp porcini powder (optional)
1 tsp rice vinegar
2 eggs
1 tsp soy sauce
2 tbsp vegetable oil
125g/4½oz portobello or
  flat mushrooms (about 2),
  thinly sliced

TO SERVE
Good drizzle of Sticky Soy Glaze
  (p. 248)

Good drizzle of Japanese Mayo
  (p. 251) or Kewpie mayo
Sprinkle of aonori or shredded
  nori (optional)
Handful of katsuobushi
  (optional)

---

**1.** Prepare the Sticky Soy Glaze (p. 248) and Japanese Mayo (p. 251). Mix the sliced cabbage with the spring onions and sushi ginger.

**2.** Mix the flour, salt, sugar, baking powder and porcini powder together.

**3.** Whisk the rice vinegar, eggs, soy sauce and 100ml/3½fl oz water in a separate bowl, then gradually mix in the dry ingredients to form a batter. Add the batter to the vegetable mix.

**4.** Cut 2 circles of baking parchment the size of your frying pan.

**5.** Heat the frying pan with 1 tablespoon of oil and place one piece of baking parchment on

the base. Pour all the batter into the pan. Add a layer of sliced mushrooms on top of the batter and, using a spatula, push any liquid that seeps out back inside the pancake. Place the second piece of parchment on top like a sandwich, add a lid and cook over a medium heat for 7–10 minutes.

**6.** Remove the lid and you should see the edges starting to turn golden brown. Turn off the heat and *very* carefully, using oven gloves or a tea towel, place a pizza tray on top of the pan, put your hand on the tray and flip the pancake onto the tray in one swift motion.

**7.** Both pieces of parchment should be sandwiching the pancake on the tray. Gently slide the pancake back into the pan, mushroom side down, and cook for a further 7–10 minutes over a medium heat with the lid off. Peel off the parchment facing upwards and add 1 tablespoon of oil around the outside to cook the pancake.

**8.** Turn off the heat and let the pancake cool inside the pan for 2 minutes before taking a large serving plate, placing it on the base of the pancake and flipping once more onto the plate.

**9.** Peel off the baking parchment to reveal the mushrooms, then double drizzle over the Sticky Soy Glaze and Japanese Mayo.

**10.** Finish with aonori and katsuobushi.

**Taste and adjust** with sauces and toppings but try not to alter the base recipe.

HOW TO MAKE OKONOMIYAKI

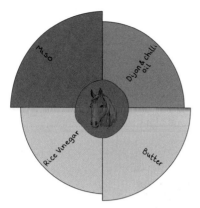

# *Fancy* Miso and Gochu Marinated Cod

You might have been to Nobu or Zuma or Sexy Fish and had a miso black cod. It's SUPER yum. With this recipe, you could be eating it more regularly. The key is marination. Marinating fish in miso is a traditional Japanese technique to preserve the fish, and because miso is a fermented product it actually draws out the natural umami from the fish and creates that beautiful flaky texture that we all dream of.

This is probably the most 'cheffy' recipe in this book, but honestly it's dead easy. I've switched up the marinade so it's got gochujang and miso, because they're both super tasty.

**SERVES 4**

**Essential Equipment**
Small whisk or stick blender; saucepan; oven tray

100g/3½oz miso
100g/3½oz gochujang
125ml/4½fl oz mirin
4 tbsp sugar
4 x 120g/4oz pieces black cod or cod

FOR THE CHILLI AND MISO SPLIT SAUCE
100g/3½oz butter
100ml/3½fl oz rice wine vinegar
1 tbsp miso
½ tbsp mustard (English or Dijon)
1 tbsp yuzu juice or lemon juice
1 ice cube (optional)
1 tsp Philli's Chilli Oil (p. 250) or shop-bought chilli oil

TO SERVE
It's great with blanched pak choi or Fennel and Cucumber Slaw (p. 196), Forbidden Black Garlic Rice (p. 242) and a side of smugness. Talk about fancy AF.

**1.** Mix the miso, gochujang, mirin and sugar to make a marinade. Marinate the fish and then put into a lidded container to marinate for a minimum of 6 hours but preferably overnight.

**2.** Remove the fish from the marinade and wipe clean. Place the fish skin side down on a lined oven tray and preheat the grill.

**3.** To make the sauce, clarify the butter. Either pop it in the microwave and cook in 30-second intervals until it's fully melted and the milk solids are separated from the fat, or heat in a saucepan until it's fully separated.

**4.** Put the vinegar in a saucepan and cook over a medium heat until it's half evaporated. Turn down the heat and whisk in the miso and mustard.

**5.** Slowly add the clarified butter until the sauce starts to thicken. Do not add the milk solids.

**6.** Finish with the yuzu juice. If the sauce doesn't thicken or it looks split, add an ice cube and gently whisk or use a stick blender to emulsify. **Taste and adjust** the sauce to your palate. Keep on the hob on the lowest setting.

**7.** Grill the fish for 10–15 minutes until it's completely golden. The marinade should prevent the fish from overcooking. The internal temperature should be 45–50°C.

**8.** Remove the fish from the oven, stir a teaspoon of chilli oil into the mustard sauce and serve.

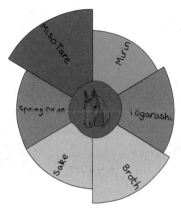

## *Fancy* Miso and Shitake Mushroom Ramen

Ramen should be a labour of love, as many ramen restaurants slave over their broths for 2–3 days. There are many recipes for a 'cheat' ramen that, though flavourful, do not stay true to a ramen recipe. However, I also realise you likely do not have the patience to watch that pot for hours on end. So there are a few shortcuts here, but you really can't tell with the end result.

A traditional ramen broth is simmered for hours to extract the pork gelatine and fat from the bones, creating a silky broth. When I was in Japan I made a visit to Tsuta, a world-famous ramen restaurant. When I ate this ramen I almost cried: beautiful tonkotsu creamy broth and a HUGE hit of truffle (I'm a sucker for truffle). The food memory has inspired this version of a shitake mushroom ramen, which extracts as much umami flavour as possible.

SERVES 4

### Essential Equipment
2 large pots; 2 saucepans; fine sieve; kitchen paper; blender

FOR THE SHITAKE DASHI BROTH
5cm/2in piece of kombu
10 dried shitake mushrooms, whole
1 tbsp katsuobushi or nutritional yeast
1 white onion, sliced
250g/9oz white mushrooms, sliced
500g/1lb 1½oz bone marrow troughs, or 2 tbsp tahini and 250ml/9fl oz oat milk
2 tbsp soy sauce, plus extra for the soy eggs

FOR THE MISO TARE
4 tbsp white miso
60ml/2fl oz sake
60ml/2fl oz mirin
Pinch of shichimi togarashi (optional)
1 tsp salt

2 eggs
1 batch fresh noodles (p. 96) or 300g/10½oz dried soba noodles
200g/7oz fresh shitake mushrooms, chopped

2 tsp truffle oil (optional)
1 small packet enoki mushrooms, chopped (optional)
2 spring onions, finely sliced
1 tsp togarashi (optional)

**1.** To make the dashi put the kombu and shitake mushrooms into a large pot with 2 litres of cold water, cover and leave at room temperature overnight or for at least 4 hours. This will extract the umami from the mushrooms and kombu.

**2.** Boil the eggs for 6½ minutes, remove and place them in iced water. Using the back of a spoon, tap all the eggshells, then peel from the top where the air gap is. Wrap each egg in kitchen paper then place in a container and soak in 3 tablespoons of soy sauce to get a marbled pattern.

Leave in the fridge overnight.

**3.** Bring the dashi broth to the boil and then add the katsuobushi or nutritional yeast, turn off the heat and cover. Leave for 45–60 minutes then strain into a jug, discarding everything except the mushrooms, and reserve the dashi separately from the mushrooms.

**4.** Put the bones in a clean pot and bring them up to the boil for 5 minutes, then strain and discard the water. Try to clean any meat or grit from the bones using a sponge. If you're using oat milk, skip this step.

**5.** Add the cleaned bones and 250ml/9fl oz water, or the oat milk and tahini, the onion and white mushrooms into the broth and bring up to a light boil and simmer for 1–2 hours. The marrow should have melted into the broth.

**6.** Remove from the heat, discard the bones, strain the vegetables and discard, then finish the broth by blending with an immersion blender and adding soy sauce and taste.

**7.** To make the miso tare, put all the ingredients in a small saucepan and simmer for 5 minutes.

**8.** Fry the reserved shitake mushrooms with the fresh shitake mushrooms in a large frying pan until golden.

**9.** Boil the noodles in a separate saucepan until just soft, about 1 minute if using fresh or to the cooking instructions if dried.

**10.** Add a tablespoon of the tare to each bowl, then add ½ teaspoon of truffle oil to each bowl with 2 ladles of broth. Strain the noodles and add to each bowl, then add a further ladle of broth, top with half a soy egg, cooked mushrooms, raw enoki mushrooms, spring onions and togarashi.

**Taste and adjust** as you eat.

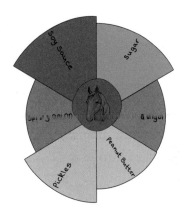

SERVES 4

**Essential Equipment**
Large wok

10g dried shitake mushrooms (optional)
800g/1lb 1½oz skin-on pork belly, cut into 1.5cm/½in pieces
25g/1oz white sugar
2 tbsp neutral oil
5cm/2in piece of ginger, sliced
3 garlic cloves, sliced
4 spring onions, white part for cooking, green for garnish, sliced
1½ tbsp light soy sauce
1½ tbsp dark soy sauce
1 tsp five-spice powder
½ tbsp peanut butter

TO SERVE
Crispy Things (p. 252)
Quick Pickled Cucs (p. 161)
Cooked short-grain rice

# Lu Rou Fan
## (Taiwanese-Inspired Braised Pork Rice Bowl)

Lu rou fan is one of the most popular dishes in Taipei and for good reason: it's fatty, rich, comforting and packed with intense soy flavours.

Now, what's the difference between light and dark soy sauce? I get asked this all the time, and because I like to keep the kitchen cupboard as simple as possible I generally only use light soy sauce, as it drives the salty flavour. Light is most versatile, often used in dressings and to add flavour. Dark soy sauce is used in braises; it's mainly for colour and sweetness, and it isn't as salty, which I always found surprising.

Once you're done with the sauce you might think it's a little fatty; if so, simply boil up the sauce and use peanut butter as an emulsifier, as Eric from 886, NYC ingeniously invented. To balance the richness of the dish, grab some pickles to brighten up the flavour.

**1.** If using shitake mushrooms, take 100ml/3½fl oz of boiling water and pour it over the dried shitake mushrooms in a heat-proof container.

**2.** Put the diced pork in a large wok or saucepan and cover with water. Simmer over a low heat for 30–40 minutes.

**3.** Remove the pork, strain through a colander and discard the water.

**4.** Wipe the wok clean and add the sugar and 1 tablespoon of water. Heat once more to allow the sugar to become a golden brown caramel.

**5.** Add 50ml/1½fl oz hot water, then pour the caramel sauce into a small container and put the wok back on the hob.

**6.** Wipe the wok clean, add the oil and the reserved pork belly. Caramelise in 2 batches for 6–7 minutes per batch until golden. Remove the pork and transfer to a plate.

**7.** Remove the shitake mushrooms from the water, keeping the water for later. Slice up the mushrooms.

**8.** Add the sliced shitake mushrooms, ginger, garlic and white part of the spring onions and fry for 3–4 minutes over a medium heat.

**9.** Add in both soy sauces and cook down for 2–3 minutes.

**10.** Add 400ml/14fl oz water, the mushroom water (from earlier), caramelised pork, five-spice and the caramel sauce that you made earlier. Allow to cook down, uncovered, over a medium heat for 30–40 minutes. You want the pork super tender and the sauce thick, just coating the pork.

**11.** Stir in the peanut butter and turn down the heat.

**12. Taste and adjust** the sauce to your palate.

**13.** Serve with the sliced green part of the spring onion with Crispy Things, Quick Pickled Cucs and steamed rice.

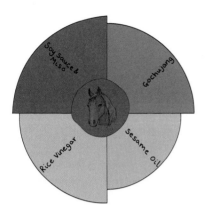

# KBBQ Bulgogi Steak

One of my favourite cuts is bavette. It's a little less utilised than sirloin or fillet and, due to the fibres, it can hold getting cooked a little longer. If you can't get hold of bavette, opt for a rump. A bulgogi marinade is soy-based, and pears are often used in Korean marinades to tenderise the meat.

SERVES 4

**Essential Equipment**
Cast-iron frying pan or heavy-based frying pan

700g/1lb 8½oz bavette steak or rump, thinly sliced
1 nashi pear or pear, grated
60ml/2fl oz soy sauce
1 tbsp brown sugar
2 tbsp sesame oil
3 garlic cloves, minced
2.5cm/1in piece of ginger, minced
1 tsp sesame seeds
2 tbsp sesame oil
4 spring onions, finely sliced

FOR THE DIPPING SAUCE
4 tbsp gochujang
1 tsp miso
3 tsp rice vinegar
1 tsp soy sauce
1 tsp sesame oil

**1.** Pop the beef in the freezer for 10 minutes while you make the marinade.

**2.** Mix together the pear, soy sauce, sugar, sesame oil, garlic, ginger and sesame seeds.

**3.** Take out the beef and use your longest, sharpest knife to slice it as thinly as you can against the grain.

**4.** Mix the beef with the marinade and leave for at least 2 hours but preferably overnight in a sealed container in the fridge.

**5.** Mix the gochujang, miso, rice vinegar, soy sauce, sesame oil and 2 tablespoons of water together to make the dipping sauce. **Taste and adjust** to your palate.

**6.** Turn on your extractor fan and heat the sesame oil in a large pan over a high heat until it's almost smoking. Remove the beef from the marinade and pat dry. Working in batches, fry the beef slices for 2–3 minutes per side, then remove. Add more sesame oil if necessary. Be careful as the sugar in the marinade can caramelise quickly.

**7.** Garnish with spring onions and serve with the dipping sauce.

# *Fancy* Forbidden Black Garlic Rice

2 tbsp olive oil, plus extra for
   drizzling
1 onion, diced
225g/8oz short-grain black rice
   (Venus or Venere) or short-
   grain brown rice (not wild rice)
4 eggs
2 tbsp any white vinegar
1 head of black garlic, cloves
   removed and blended, or
   2 tbsp paste
2 tbsp butter
1 tbsp gochujang
60ml/2fl oz soy sauce
Juice of ½ lemon
Handful of chopped chives

TO SERVE
Cheat XO Sauce (p. 255) or Philli's
   Chilli Oil (p. 250)

In ancient China black rice was also known as forbidden rice because it was super expensive and only the upper class could afford it. In acupuncture and Chinese medicine, it's thought that black rice regulates appetite, strengthens your liver and improves vision, so if you like a glass of wine or didn't eat your carrots as a child it's not too late. It's also packed with antioxidants – finally, a carb that tastes good and is good for you too. Please don't confuse this with wild rice, which does not taste good (personal opinion).

Luckily, today black rice is more readily available and the majority of what we see is a crossbreed between Asian black rice and Italian short grain. It's a little nutty and chewy and super yum.

You'll be flavouring the rice with black garlic. Black garlic starts its life as normal garlic but is fermented. You can do this at home if you have a rice cooker; in a keep warm setting it normally takes 9 days. Be warned: it can get smelly, so I prefer to get it at my local supermarket.

**1.** Heat the olive oil in a saucepan over a medium heat. Add the onion and cook until caramelised, about 2–3 minutes.

**2.** Add the black rice and 480ml/17fl oz water.

**3.** Bring to the boil and cover with a lid, turn down the heat and cook for 30 minutes or until the water is absorbed.

**4.** Poach the eggs in a saucepan of simmering water with the vinegar added. Swirl the water and add the eggs from a ramekin. Cook the eggs two at a time for 2–3 minutes for each egg, remove with a slotted spoon and drain on a J-cloth. Trim any excess from the eggs.

**5.** Once the rice is cooked, turn off the heat and allow to stand for 5 minutes.

**6.** Add the black garlic, butter, gochujang and soy sauce and mix through.

**7.** Finish with a squeeze of lemon and a sprinkle of chives, **taste and adjust** to your palate.

**8.** Serve the rice in bowls and make a well in the middle for the egg to sit in.

**9.** Drizzle XO sauce or chilli oil over each egg and enjoy.

# Miso Sticky Toffee Pudding ⓥ

STP (sticky toffee pudding) is a classic. When I was younger my grandparents lived in the Lake District and we'd always make a stop off at Cartmel for an STP. I loved the intensely sweet date pudding but it was the super sweet treacle sauce I could never get enough of. Probably why I have to make so many trips to the dentist.

I wanted to make this classic a little more me and grown up by adding a bit of miso and whisky. Although it's my least favourite alcohol, this one is for my dad.

SERVES 8

**Essential Equipment**
23 x 33cm/9 x 13in baking tin; stick blender; stand mixer (preferably) or hand whisk

FOR THE SPONGE
250g/9oz soft dried pitted dates, roughly chopped
1½ tsp bicarbonate of soda
130g/4½oz unsalted butter, softened, plus extra for greasing
75g/2½oz dark brown sugar
3 large eggs, at room temperature
225g/8oz plain flour
3 tsp baking powder

FOR THE WHISKY MISO SAUCE
100g/3½oz unsalted butter, softened
200g/7oz dark brown sugar
200ml/7fl oz double cream
1 tbsp miso
2 tbsp whisky (optional)

**1.** Preheat the oven to 180°C (160°C fan oven) Gas 4 and line your baking tin with baking parchment.

**2.** Mix the dates and bicarb with 300ml/11fl oz water from a freshly boiled kettle and leave for 20 minutes. (The bicarb breaks down the cellulose of the dates, making them softer.)

**3.** In a stand mixer, beat together the butter and sugar.

**4.** Add in one egg at a time, and mix together.

**5.** Slow the mixer down. Mix together the flour and baking powder and add a couple of tablespoons at a time until all the flour is incorporated.

**6.** Blend the dates and water using a stick blender and then add them into the batter.

**7.** Pour the mix into the tin and bake for 30–35 minutes until a skewer comes out clean.

**8.** To make the sauce, melt the butter and sugar in a saucepan on low until fully melted.

**9.** Add the cream, turn the heat to high and cook until it's deep in colour and very bubbly.

**10.** Take off the heat and stir in the miso and whisky.

**11. Taste and adjus**t to your palate. If you want to, add a little more whisky or miso to add a touch of savoury.

**12.** Take the cake out of the oven and use a skewer or a fork to prick it all over.

**13.** Leaving the cake in the tin, drench it in half the miso caramel sauce.

**14.** Cover the tin in foil and keep warm. You can bake this ahead of time and then simply pop it back into the oven for 10 minutes

**15.** Cut into squares and serve with more whisky miso sauce.

# THE SAUCE

Condiments make a dish and I love to have a selection
in my cupboards and fridge. You can make these beforehand and
use them in your everyday recipes as well as to level up
your pizza night dipping sauces.

# Kiddish sauces

## SRIRACHA HOT HONEY

I love hot honey on pizzas but why stop there? What's not to love about spice and sweet? It's great for dunking nuggz or chippies.

4 tbsp honey
4 tbsp sriracha or Funky Chilli Sauce (opposite)
Juice of 1 lime

**1.** Mix all the ingredients together into a thick glaze and use.

**2.** Store in an airtight container for up to a week.

## BUTTERY KOREAN BBQ SAUCE (KBBQ SAUCE)

Okay, okay, by now I hope you can also come to LOVE gochujang. This is my favourite Korean BBQ sauce because it's somewhere between a buffalo sauce and a traditional Korean BBQ sauce, and holds the perfect glaze.

1 tbsp sesame oil
2 garlic cloves, minced
2.5cm/1in piece of ginger, minced
4 tbsp gochujang
4 tbsp ketchup
4 tbsp honey
4 tbsp brown sugar
2 tbsp rice wine vinegar
2 tbsp soy sauce
50g/1½oz butter

**1.** Fry the garlic and ginger in sesame oil in a small saucepan for 2–3 minutes over a medium heat.

**2.** Add the gochujang, ketchup, honey, brown sugar, rice wine vinegar and soy and stir together.

**3.** Before serving, whisk in the butter over a low heat; you may need a tablespoon of water to loosen the sauce.

**4.** Store in an airtight container for up to a week, and reheat in the microwave or in a saucepan over a low heat.

## STICKY SOY GLAZE

Kejap manis is a super intense, sweet, sticky Indonesian soy sauce. I love it, but it's sometimes hard to find. Fear not! You can make your own with just two ingredients. Whack it on some rice like the Egg and Bacon Nasi Goreng (p. 138) – super delish!

50g/1½oz brown sugar
50ml/1½fl oz dark soy sauce

**1.** Heat the soy sauce and sugar in a saucepan over a low heat for 5–10 minutes until just thickened. It'll continue to thicken as it cools. Don't overcook it, otherwise you'll get caramel.

**2.** Allow to cool to room temperature and store in an airtight container.

# Spice Master sauces

## FUNKY CHILLI SAUCE

I wouldn't normally make my own chilli sauces as there are some great options to buy off the shelf; however, I do love a chilli oil and a funky fermented chilli sauce. These two are my ultimate hot sauces which I always have at the ready to spice up any dish.

20 chillies (I like a mix of
    3 scotch bonnets, 10 bird's eye,
    7 red chillies)
1½ tsp/10g salt
10 cherry tomatoes
3 garlic cloves
200ml/7fl oz mineral water
2 carrots
1 tbsp neutral oil, plus 100ml
    for blending
Juice of 1 lime
75ml/2½fl oz malt vinegar
1 tbsp honey
½ tsp salt, extra

**1.** Blend the chillies, salt, cherry tomatoes, garlic and mineral water into a fine paste. Then pop everything in a sterilised jar and cover with a cheesecloth or a clean face mask and leave to ferment at room temperature for 1–3 days. You should start to see little bubbles form.

**2.** Preheat the oven to 180°C (160°C fan oven) Gas 4.

**3.** Peel and roughly chop the carrots and drizzle with 1 tablespoon of neutral oil.

**4.** Roast for 20 minutes or until soft.

**5.** Put the fermented chilli paste in a blender with the lime juice, vinegar, honey, carrots and extra salt and oil. Blend until fully smooth, then strain through a sieve.

**6.** Transfer to a bottle and keep it at room temperature for a further 2–3 days. Keep opening the bottle each day to burp the sauce and **taste** it. It'll become more acidic and funkier the longer you leave it.

**7.** Once you are happy with the flavour, store the sauce in the fridge for up to a month.

## PHILLI'S CHILLI OIL

There are many chilli oils from across China. Some of the most famous are Chiu Chow, chilli crisp, Sichuan and XO sauce. In Japanese cooking, there's rayu; in Malay kitchens there's belecan and don't forget the Vietnamese Sa Tế. I have taken inspiration from all of these styles and made my own type of chilli oil. I use it on everything, literally, from noods, eggs and dumplings to curries and pizza.

115ml/4fl oz neutral oil
½ tsp Sichuan peppercorns, ground
2 star anise (optional)
1 cinnamon stick (optional)
1 tbsp Sichuan chilli flakes or red chilli flakes
1 tbsp gochugaru or 1 tbsp chilli powder
4 garlic cloves, minced
2 spring onions, sliced
1 tbsp tomato paste
1 tsp sesame seeds
½ tbsp sugar
1 tbsp soy sauce

**1.** To a saucepan add half of the oil, the Sichuan peppercorns, star anise and cinnamon (if using). Heat to 110–120°C.

**2.** Put all the chilli flakes and the gochugaru into a heatproof metal bowl. Once the oil is hot, pour it with the whole spices over the chilli flakes. The oil will bubble (enjoy the ASMR!). Allow the oil to cool slightly.

**3.** Wipe the pan clean of any residue and pour in the remaining oil. Add the spring onions. Gradually heat, stirring until they become golden and crisp, about 10–15 minutes over a medium-low heat.

**4.** Add the garlic and tomato paste and sesame seeds and stir for 5 minutes. Remove the tomato garlic oil from the heat and add it to the previous chilli oil. Once the oil is cool enough to touch, **taste** and finish with sugar and soy sauce.

**5.** Store in an airtight jar and leave the cinnamon and star anise to infuse, but do not eat these when using. Store the oil at room temperature for 2 weeks or in the fridge for up to 3 months.

# Comfort sauces

### CASHEW AND TAMARIND CHUTNEY

100g/3½oz cashews
200ml/7fl oz milk or oat milk
2 tbsp tamarind
½ tsp salt

**1.** To make this creamy cashew dressing, simply simmer the cashews in milk for 30 minutes or until soft over a low heat, then blend with the tamarind paste and salt. You may need to adjust with a little more milk if the pan dries out, or in the blender to get a double cream consistency.

### JAPANESE MAYO

2 pasteurised egg yolks
2 tsp Dijon mustard
2 tbsp rice vinegar
200–250ml/7–9fl oz neutral-
    flavoured oil
1 tsp salt
2–4 tsp sugar

**1.** Whisk together the egg yolks, Dijon and rice vinegar.

**2.** Slowly add in the neutral oil and keep whisking until thick.

**3.** Season with salt and sugar.

**Tip**
If your mayo splits, add a small amount of ice to it to try and stabilise it, as this is an oil-in-water emulsion. If it all goes south following this, simply remove the split sauce, clean and dry the bowl and whisk, add a new egg yolk then whisk in the split sauce to your new yolk until it comes together.

### TAHINI SOY SAUCE

4 tbsp tahini
2 tbsp rice wine vinegar
1 tbsp soy sauce

**1.** Mix together the tahini and rice wine vinegar until thick.

**2.** Slowly mix in the soy sauce, then add 1 tablespoon of water at a time until the sauce reaches a double cream consistency.

## CRISPY THINGS

2 shallots
100ml/3½fl oz oil

**1.** Slice the shallots super thin (do this with a mandoline for precision but be careful and always use a guard).

**2.** Put the oil in a small frying pan and add the shallots. Slowly heat the oil and keep turning the shallots.

**3.** Keep slowly cooking until the shallots are golden.

**4.** Remove them from the oil and drain on kitchen paper.

**5.** Store in a sealed container at room temperature.

## NO-COOK SATAY SAUCE

3 tbsp smooth peanut butter
1 tbsp soy sauce
Juice of 1 lime
2 tsp brown sugar
1 tbsp fish sauce or dark
   soy sauce
1 tbsp sriracha

**1.** Make the satay sauce by whisking up all the ingredients together.

**2.** Loosen with 2–3 tablespoons of water as necessary.

# Tarty sauces

## PONZU

100ml/3½fl oz rice vinegar
2 tbsp soy sauce
4 tbsp mirin or 3 tbsp honey
1 lemon, peel and juice
1 lime, peel and juice
1 tbsp yuzu juice (optional)
10cm/4in piece of kombu
(optional)

**1.** Peel the peel off the lemon
and lime using a Y-shaped
peeler, then squeeze the juice
from both.

**2.** Mix the citrus peel and
juice with all the remaining
ingredients and store in an
airtight container overnight.

**3.** Remove the kombu and peels
and discard. Keep this sauce for
up to 2 weeks.

## NUOC CHAM

4 tbsp sugar
2 garlic clove, minced
2 bird's eye chillies or Thai
  chillies, finely sliced
Juice of 3–4 limes
4 tbsp fish sauce

**1.** Put the sugar, garlic and
chillies in a bowl and pour over
150ml/5½fl oz boiling water.
Stir and make sure all the sugar
is dissolved.

**2.** Add the lime juice and fish
sauce.

# Refined sauces

## GREEN COCONUT CHUTNEY

30g/1oz desiccated coconut
¼ red onion, sliced
2 garlic cloves, chopped
1 tbsp neutral oil
Pinch of salt
25g/1oz fresh coriander
  (about 1 small bunch)
2 green chillies, chopped
¼ tsp ground turmeric
½ tsp ground cumin
1 tbsp tamarind paste
2 tsp brown sugar or jaggery

**1.** Soak the desiccated coconut in 100ml/3½fl oz just-boiled water for 20 minutes.

**2.** In a small saucepan, cook off the onions and garlic with the oil and a pinch of salt over a medium heat until lightly coloured.

**3.** Add the onion-garlic mix to the coconut with the rest of the spices, tamarind and brown sugar in a blender or jug, blend until entirely smooth. You can keep this chutney in the fridge for up to 4 days in a sealed container.

## GREEN NAM JIM

1 garlic clove, minced
1 bunch of coriander stalks,
  sliced
1 tbsp fish sauce or ½ tbsp
  soy sauce
½ tsp dark brown sugar or
  palm sugar
Juice of 3–4 limes
2 green Thai chillies

**1.** Whack all the ingredients except the chillies into a small blender and blitz until watery and smooth. Slice the chillies and mix through. Taste and adjust to your palate.

**2.** If you're using a pestle and mortar, grind the chillies, garlic and coriander stalks to a smooth paste. Add the sugar and fish sauce and smush together. Mix in the lime juice and **taste adjust**. This sauce is spicy, salty and very sour.

# Dark Horse sauces

## SHOYU TARE

**This recipe is for the classic tare, what we often call teriyaki sauce.**

200ml/7fl oz sake
200ml/7fl oz mirin
30g/1oz sugar
100ml/3½fl oz soy sauce (preferably Japanese)

**1.** Pour the sake and mirin into a saucepan and bring to the boil, then turn down the heat and simmer for 20 minutes.

**2.** Add the sugar and cook for a further 20 minutes before adding the soy and cooking for 10 minutes. Stir, then remove from the heat and store in a heatproof, airtight container.

## CHEAT XO SAUCE

**I love this on eggs, pasta and corn – check the Cheesy Miso XO Corn (p. 230). XO sauce was invented in the 1980s in Hong Kong, where all the most expensive ingredients were combined in a sauce. They also happen to be super umami.**

25g/1oz dried mushrooms
Large pinch of katsuobushi
15g/½oz dried prawns (optional) or double katsuobushi
2.5cm/1in piece of ginger
3 garlic cloves
2 shallots or ½ onion
4 bird's eye chillies
200ml/7fl oz veg oil
80g/3oz Parma ham, torn
5 dried Chinese chillies, crushed, or 1 tbsp chilli flakes
1 tsp Sichuan peppercorns, crushed
60ml/2fl oz Shaoxing wine
250ml/9fl oz chicken stock
60ml/2fl oz oyster sauce
30ml/1fl oz soy sauce
30g/1oz sugar
2 star anise (optional)
Pinch of MSG (optional)

**1.** Add the mushrooms, katsuobushi and prawns to 200ml/7fl oz boiled water. Allow them to soften completely, then strain and blend until roughly chopped. Remove from the blender and reserve. Keep the liquid as it's great for cooking rice.

**2.** Put the ginger, garlic cloves, shallots and fresh chillies into the blender and whizz until finely chopped but not paste-like.

**3.** Heat the veg oil to 120°C, add the Parma ham and fry until crispy.

**4.** Add the mushroom katsuobushi prawn mix and fry for 2 more minutes.

**5.** Add the blended ginger, garlic, shallots and chillies and keep stirring for 5 minutes.

**6.** Add the crushed chillies and Sichuan peppercorns and cook for 2 minutes.

**7.** Pour in the Shaoxing wine and allow to simmer for 5 minutes.

**8.** Add the chicken stock, oyster sauce, soy sauce, sugar and star anise (if using) and allow to simmer for 12–15 minutes. Finish with a pinch of MSG, if you like, for an extra umami boost.

# Meal suggestions and timings

## Everyday cooking

### READY IN 15 MINUTES

Sticky Sriracha Salmon

Smoking Hot Noods (using shop-bought noods)

Tteok-Bokki (Korean-Inspired Spicy Cheesy Rice Cakes)

Red Pepper and Kimchi Rigatoni

Smacked Sichuan and Black Vinegar Cucumber

Fennel and Cucumber Slaw

Cantonese-Style Steamed Fish

Green Curry Mussels

Cheesy Miso XO Corn

Egg and Bacon Nasi Goreng (Indonesian-Inspired Fried Rice)

### READY IN 30 MINUTES OR LESS

Tamarind and Lime Glazed Salmon

Black Pepper Portobello, Charred Peppers and Watercress Salad

Vietnamese-Inspired Caramelised Pork Bowls

BBBR (Brown Butter Basmati Rice)

Satay Prawns

Cuddly Dan Dan Noods

Smacked Sichuan and Black Vinegar Cucumber

Crispy Tofu Nuggz and Green Nam Jim

Sea Bass Filipino-Inspired Kinilaw

Thai Basil Beef Steaks

Pork Larb

Mango and Thai Basil Pulled Chicken Flatbreads

Gunpowder Pots

**READY IN 1 HOUR**

Peshwari Crust Cauli Korma

Miso Honey Slow-Roast Celeriac and Cavolo Nero

Bun Thit Nuong (Vietnamese-Style Grilled Pork and Noodles)

Beetroot Lentil Mapo Tofu

Aubergine Vindaloo

Sichuan Fragrant Aubergine Tenders

The Secret Katsu Dunkers

Khao Soi (Northern Chiang Mai Curry Noodles)

Citrus Marinated Tomatoes with Garlicky Oil and Crispy Chapatis

Filipino-Inspired Chicken Adobo

Goan-Inspired Prawn and Crab Curry with Blistered Tomatoes

Coriander and Coconut Chicken Curry

Mango and Thai Basil Pulled Chicken Flatbreads

Shitake Okonomiyaki

Fish Sauce Chicken Wings

KBBQ Bulgogi Steak

Forbidden Black Garlic Rice

**MAKE AHEAD**

Hong Kong-Style Pork Belly

Women of Shaolin Cabbage Dumplings with Sesame Dressing

Sausage Meat Wontons with the Perfect Dumpling Dressing

My Squishy Bao

Short Rib Rendang with Beef Dripping Crispy Potatoes

Sichuan Lamb Chops with Chilli Oil Crispy Potatoes

Miso and Wild Mushroom Ramen

Soy-Glazed King Oyster Mushroom 'Murger' Pitas

Lu Rou Fan (Taiwanese Braised Pork Rice Bowl)

Miso Sticky Toffee Pudding

Japanese Cheesecake

# Occasion

## EAT SOLO

**(reduce quantities to serve 1 or keep a portion in the fridge for later)**

Sticky Sriracha Salmon (fillets)

Smoking Hot Noods

Black Bean Makhani

Red Pepper and Kimchi Rigatoni

Cuddly Dan Dan Noods

Egg and Bacon Nasi Goreng (Indonesian-Inspired Fried Rice)

## SOMETHING TO WOW

Peshwari Crust Cauli Korma

Korean Fried Chicken Burger

Short Rib Rendang with Beef Dripping Crispy Potatoes

Tuna Tataki with Gomae Dressing

Goan-Inspired Prawn and Crab Curry with Blistered Tomatoes

Thai Basil Beef Steaks

Shitake Okonomiyaki

Miso and Gochu Marinated Cod

## SICK SIDES

Maple and Sesame Glazed Carrots

My Mum's Chapatis

BBBR (Brown Butter Basmati Rice)

My Squishy Bao

Smacked Sichuan and Black Vinegar Cucumber

Gunpowder Pots

Garlicky Oniony Flaky Pancake

Smoky Hispi Cabbage with Chilli Oil

Fennel and Cucumber Slaw

Charred Broccoli, Balsamic Red Onions and Tahini Soy Sauce

Crispy Kale and Squash with Satay Sauce

Cheesy Miso XO Corn

Forbidden Black Garlic Rice

## SOMETHING TO SHARE

Satay Prawns

Brown Butter, Biscoff and Miso Blondies

Korean Chilli No-Knead Focaccia

Raging Chilli Paneer Puffs with Rocket Chilli and Lemon Yog

Citrus Marinated Tomatoes with Garlicky Oil and Crispy Chapatis

Crispy Tofu Nuggz and Green Nam Jim

Sea Bass Filipino-Inspired Kinilaw

Spicy Green Fish Cakes

Chicken Yakitori with Togarashi Spice

Soy-Glazed King Oyster Mushroom 'Murger' Pitas

Fish Sauce Chicken Wings

## WEEKNIGHT CLASSICS

Sticky Sriracha Salmon

Vietnamese-Inspired Caramelised Pork Bowls

Black Bean Makhani

Sichuan Fragrant Aubergine Tenders

Red Pepper and Kimchi Rigatoni

The Secret Katsu Dunkers

Cuddly Dan Dan Noods

Egg and Bacon Nasi Goreng (Indonesian-Inspired Fried Rice)

Tamarind and Lime Glazed Salmon

Filipino-Inspired Chicken Adobo

Coriander and Coconut Chicken Curry

Mango and Thai Basil Pulled Chicken Flatbreads

Pork Larb

## BRUNCH

Halloumi and Baked Cherry Toms with Hot Honey Drizzle

Korean Chilli No-Knead Foccaccia

## SUMMER DISHES

Sticky Sriracha Salmon

Bun Thit Nuong (Vietnamese-Style Grilled Pork and Noodles)

Sea Bass Filipino-Inspired Kinilaw

Cantonese-Style Steamed Fish

Green Curry Mussels

KBBQ Bulgogi Steak

## SUNDAY ROASTS

Peshwari Crust Cauli Korma

Hong Kong-Style Pork Belly

Gochujang Spatchcock Chicken and Duck Fat Spicy Roasties

Sichuan Lamb Chops with Chilli Oil Crispy Potatoes

Short Rib Rendang with Beef Dripping Crispy Potatoes

## WINTER WARMERS

Miso Honey Slow-Roast Celeriac and Cavolo Nero

Tteok-Bokki (Korean-Inspired Spicy Cheesy Rice Cakes)

Beetroot Lentil Mapo Tofu

Black Bean Makhani

Red Pepper and Kimchi Rigatoni

Cuddly Dan Dan Noods

Egg and Bacon Nasi Goreng (Indonesian-Inspired Fried Rice)

The Secret Katsu Dunkers

Khao Soi (Northern Chiang Mai Curry Noodles)

Lu Rou Fan (Taiwanese Braised Pork Rice Bowl)

Short Rib Rendang with Beef Dripping Crispy Potatoes

## POWER PUDS

Brown Butter, Biscoff and Miso Blondies

Japanese Cheesecake

Watermelon and Wasabi Snow Cone with Lime

Mango Crumble and Chai Custard

Fuss-Free Yuzu Lemon Tart(ish) with Sichuan Poached Rhubarb

1-Ingredient Dark Chocolate Pots and Raspberry Jam

Miso Sticky Toffee Pudding

# Menu ideas to impress

## VEGAN MENUS

Citrus Marinated Tomatoes with Garlicky Oil and Crispy Chapatis

Aubergine Vindaloo

Watermelon and Wasabi Snow Cone with Lime

———

Maple and Sesame Glazed Carrots

Soy-Glazed King Oyster Mushroom 'Murger' Pitas

1-Ingredient Dark chocolate Pots with Raspberry Jam

———

## VEGGIE MENUS

Black Bean Makhani

Peshwari Crust Cauli Korma

BBBR (Brown Butter Basmati Rice)

Miso Sticky Toffee Pudding

———

Smoky Hispi Cabbage with Chilli Oil

Shitake Okonomiyaki

Japanese Cheesecake

## FISH MENUS

Sea Bass Filipino-Inspired Kinilaw

Goan-Inspired Prawn and Crab Curry with Blistered Tomatoes

BBBR (Brown Butter Basmati Rice)

Cashew and Tamarind Chutney

Green Coconut Chutney

My Mum's Chapatis

———

Green Curry Mussels

Gunpowder Pots

Mango Crumble and Chai Custard

———

## MEATY MENUS

Spicy Green Fish Cakes

Sichuan Lamb Chops with Chilli Oil Crispy Potatoes

Watermelon and Wasabi Snow Cone with Lime

———

KBBQ Bulgogi Steak

Miso and Gochu Marinated Cod

Fuss-Free Yuzu Lemon Tart(ish) with Sichuan Poached Rhubarb

# My ultimate menus

Green Curry Mussels with
Garlicky Oniony Flaky Pancake

Short Rib Rendang with Beef
Dripping Crispy Potatoes

Miso Sticky Toffee Pudding

———

My Squishy Bao filled with Hong
Kong-Style Pork Belly

Quick Pickled Cucs

How I Kimchi

Smoky Hispi Cabbage with
Chilli Oil

Cheesy Miso XO Corn

Gunpowder Pots

———

Peshwari Crust Cauli Korma

Black Bean Makhani

Goan-Inspired Prawn and Crab
Curry with Blistered Tomatoes

My Mum's Chapatis

BBBR (Brown Butter Basmati
Rice)

———

Shitake Okonomiyaki

Miso and Gochu Marinated Cod

Japanese Cheesecake

# Further Reading

## FOOD SCIENCE

Jopson, Marty, *The Science of Food: An Exploration of What We Eat and How We Cook* (Michael O'Mara, 2017)

Katz, Sandor Ellix, *The Art of Fermentation* (Chelsea Green Publishing Co, 2009)

López-Alt, J. Kenji, *The Food Lab: Better Home Cooking Through Science* (W. W. Norton & Company, 2015)

Mcgee, Harold, *McGee on Food and Cooking: An Encyclopedia of Kitchen Science, History and Culture* (Hodder & Stoughton, 2004)

Mcgee, Harold, *Nose Dive: A Field Guide to the World's Smells* (John Murray, 2020)

Nosrat, Samin, *Salt, Fat, Acid, Heat: Mastering the Elements of Good Cooking* (Canongate Books, 2017)

Spence, Charles, *Gastrophysics: The New Science of Eating* (Viking, 2017)

## FLAVOUR PAIRING BOOKS I LOVE

Fleischman, Adam, *Flavor Bombs: The Umami Ingredients That Make Taste Explode* (Rux Martin / Houghton Mifflin Harcourt, 2018)

Ottolenghi, Yotam and Belfrage, Ixta, *Flavour* (Ebury Press, 2020)

Ottolenghi, Yotam, *Test Kitchen: Shelf Love* (Ebury Press, 2021)

Segnit, Niki, *The Flavour Thesaurus* (Bloomsbury, 2010)

Smith, Ed, *Crave: Recipes Arranged by Flavour, to Suit Your Mood and Appetite* (Quadrille Publishing Ltd, 2021)

## ASIAN SPECIALITY BOOKS I LOVE

Chang, Dave, *Momofuku* (Absolute Press, 2010)

Dunlop, Fuschia, *The Food of Sichuan* (Bloomsbury, 2019)

Wang, Jason, *Xi'an Famous Foods* (Abrams, 2020)

Ford, Eleanor, *Fire Islands: Recipes from Indonesia* (Murdoch Books, 2019)

Middlehurst, Pippa, *Dumplings and Noodles: Bao, Gyoza, Biang Biang, Ramen – and Everything in Between* (Quadrille Publishing Ltd, 2020)

Tsuji, Shizuo, *Japanese Cooking: A Simple Art* (Kodansha Amer Inc, 2012)

Murota, Maori, *Tokyi Cult Recipes* (Murdoch Books, 2015)

Shah, Santosh, *Ayla: A Feast of Nepali Dishes from Terai, Hills and the Himalayas* (DK, 2022)

Anderson, Tim, *Japaneasy* (Hardie Grant, 2017)

# Acknowledgements

## BIG THANK YOU

First of all, I would love to say one massive thank you to you. Without your support I would not be a published author releasing my very own cookbook and sharing the food I love! Thank you for being as interested in flavour as I am, and nerding out with the food science so that the dream of writing this cookbook becomes a reality.

To all the Taste Kitchen Testers, for testing out all the recipes and exchanging endless WhatsApp messages, you've made me feel so much closer to everyone who cooks my food. You guys rock.

THANK YOU TO ...

...the whole Little, Brown team and the wider Hachette group, especially Tom Asker, for taking a chance on me and editing my weird language to make it so much more readable. Alison Griffiths for correcting all my spelling mistakes, and making the book flow.

...Phoebe Pearson, thank you for your bundles of energy, and pushing the photos to the next level, and having crazy idea sessions – I have a new appreciation for exactly where that coriander leaf should be placed.

...Megan Thomson, for picking the ultimate props and taking our photos to the next level, and lifting the energy and mood.

...Lucas Pelizaro, for videoing and editing all the skill videos and being overall lovely.

...Milli Collins, for drawing the beautiful illustrations and bringing my crazy vision to life.

...Bekki Guyatt, for designing this EPIC front cover.

...Andrew Barron, for making these book pages beaut.

...Edd Gold, and the gold studios for your continued support and guiding me in writing the book.

...Heather Holden-Brown, my literary agent, for liaising with the Little, Brown team.

...Valda Goodfellow, for loaning plates for the shoot and your ongoing support.

...Carla Risdon, for loaning me the beautiful aprons.

...Ren, Rex and Angelo; for teaching about your food culture.

...Charles Spence and Peter Barham and all my heroes in Food Science, for being such a great influence to this book and my passion.

...Mum and Dad, for your continued support and allowing me to always feel like I am able to do anything I set my mind to.

Lastly, thank you, Tom – I couldn't have achieved any of this without you, you give me the ability to do what I love. I can't thank you enough. (Also the endless supermarket trips hero.)

# Index

**SHARPEN YOUR KNIFE**

**MAKE PUFFY JUICY PORK BELLY**

**MAKE JAPANESE CHEESECAKE BATTER**

**ROLL RICE CAKES**

**FOLD FOCACCIA**

**MAKE NOODLES**

**SPATCHCOCK A CHICKEN**

**ROLL CHAPATIS**

**ROLL AND FOLD DUMPLINGS**

**DE-POOP PRAWNS**

**MAKE BAO**

**PREPARE SHORT RIB**

**SLICE TUNA**

**ROLL FLAKY PANCAKES**

**STEAM FISH IN PARCHMENT**

**SIZZLE THAT STEAK**

**PREPARE CHICKEN SKEWERS**

**MAKE PITAS**

**MAKE OKONOMIYAKI**

**THE WHOOPSIES**

ROBINSON

First published in Great Britain in 2022
by Robinson

10 9 8 7 6 5 4 3 2 1

A CIP catalogue record for this book is available
from the British Library.

ISBN 978-1-47214-727-1

Typeset in Fira Sans

Printed and bound in Italy by L.E.G.O S.p.A

Papers used by Robinson are from
well-managed forests and other
responsible sources.

Robinson
An imprint of Little, Brown Book Group
Carmelite House
50 Victoria Embankment
London EC4Y 0DZ

An Hachette UK Company
www.hachette.co.uk

www.littlebrown.co.uk

THANK YOU